The Birth of a Rican

Manuel Hernandez Carmona

The Birth of a Rican

Copyright © 2021 Manuel Hernandez Carmona

Front cover design and rights: Dr. Maria Victoria Torrey

ISBN: 979-8455429293 (Paperback)

Printed in the United States of America

FOREWORD
Dr. Maria Victoria Torrey

Awareness of one's Puerto Rican Identity is as important today as it has been for decades in the United States, particularly regarding literature. Words are powerful, evoking images and ultimately contributing to one's identity. Inferiority issues (or vice versa) usually result from how, or what, one thinks about themselves. In my doctoral dissertation, "Puerto Rican Authors: Voicing Identity in Puerto Rican Literature", I presented issues of identity representing people living dualities across many cultural crossroads (literature, language, music, food, etc.). I began the journey to understand my Puerto Rican identity when I researched it in San Francisco, after having lived more than two decades as a "Hispanic" versus a "Boricua." My Boricua Identity continues to evolve as I delve into the stories and the histories that contributed to my nature and nurture as a human being.

Mimetic of my personal journey as a Boricua scholar, teacher, activist, writer/publisher and friend, Mr. Hernandez, shares my passion for writing that proposes a sense of self-affirmation and personal involvement: an ideology that blends stories that have the potential to inspire others to value their own identities, consequently sharing them via published narratives. Adolescent students are motivated by the inclusion of their culture in the materials used that address the formation of identity and meaning that supports the development of the "Latino", Hispanic or Boricua youth in such a critical developmental period.

Meeting Mr. Hernandez during his "Florida Experience", added to this second edition of the book, posed an opportunity that sparked a renewed focus for my research. In years prior, conversations fell short of action, because local school board curricular restrictions prioritize predetermined themes emanating from textbook chapters. Nevertheless, the textbook themes are usually broad enough to supplement a topic with supplementary materials that are high interest, such as compact books consisting of learning strategies and vocabulary schema embedded from the cultural context of the book.

Each chapter in Mr. Hernández' book provided opportunities for students to read, appreciate and reflect on their own culture. Unlike stereotypes in other published sources, when one can perceive or access oneself positively in literature, a healthy emotional connection can be established that takes root in a young, developing mind, before and during the tender adolescent years. While using the book in my classroom, exciting learning resulted from students' reading experiences, which ended with a journal project and a visit from the author! Students benefited from the interaction with the author; they asked questions that were relevant to the dynamic identities that were represented in the classroom.

A foundational tenet that informs my personal educational philosophy emphasizes the concept of "Authors in the Classroom," which inspire principles that enrich student identities and encourages shared stories to be published via individual or group narratives. I was fortunate to find such a colleague with similar beliefs and aspirations, paralleling my journey as an educator and promoting cultural identity for all students. Eventually we collaborated, and my investment of a class-set of the first edition of his book for my students enabled me to write curriculum and implement lessons that supplemented state-adopted materials, as well as aligning Florida curriculum standards.

In "The Birth of a Rican, "Manolo" portrays my colleague's experiences that mirror the reality of Puerto Ricans on the U.S. mainland, as well as in California and Hawaii. In Puerto Rico, multiple racial and cultural identities had intermingled due to the traffic flow throughout this politically strategic island in the Caribbean during the colonial era, which included the African slave trade. In 1917, Puerto Ricans became citizens of the U.S., which changed the political status of the Puerto Rican and led to facilitating the back-and-forth movement of the "Rican". The term is defined in the Internet Urban Dictionary as an American offspring, born of Puerto Rican-born parents (or ancestors), who may or may not have ever visited the island. Ricans are in constant flux, with identities nurtured by generational interactions that take place between the life of the individual and their social setting, whether they resided on or off the island.

My own background is as a Rican, born in a multi-ethnic neighborhood in Manhattan's Lower East Side in New York, not far from "Losaida" a Puerto Rican neighborhood that hosts "The Nuyorican Poet's Café. Initially considered a derogatory term, I believed that the term "Nuyorican" insulted me and marginalized my status as a United States citizen; I rejected it as a desired identity. Overtime, I eventually embraced the connotation that came along with the term, because of the intellectual value of the literature that thrived with relevant content. Cultural connections had been missing from my life, after living far away from the cultural ties that helped to form my identity. My longing to understand meaningful family relationships, ethnic or racial-identity neighborhood characteristics, migration issues, social justice, acculturation, among other emotional connections moves me to support and promote Mr. Hernandez' "Birth of a Rican."

TABLE OF CONTENTS

Foreword   3

A Typical American Boy   9

Growing up in Two Worlds   26

The Umbrella Factory   33

My Bachelor's Degree   42

Getting Ahead   51

Coming Home   58

Ground Zero   65

The Florida Experience   96

About the Author   113

About the Graphic Artist and Author   114

A TYPICAL AMERICAN BOY

Manuel and Carmen came to the United States of America in the early 1950's. The Caribbean island called Puerto Rico has one of the highest rates of emigration in the world. Puerto Ricans began migrating to the United States as early as the mid-eighteenth century, but it was not until after World War II that their presence as a community developed. My folks were part of a massive immigration movement inspired by the new Puerto Rican Commonwealth Government of 1952 and its strong political and economic ties to the United States, and they joined thousands of compatriots and other worldwide immigrants in the quest of the American Dream.

Father was born during the height of the Great Depression in 1938. As a United States territory, Puerto Rico participated in the financial debacle of the era. Living on the Island was hard, and there were a lot of people without work. He was the second born in a family of seven. My grandparents separated when dad was five years old. Grandfather had dreams of a better life in the United States, and grandmother wanted more rice and beans on the plate. After Ramona, Manolín, Modesto, Félix and Toño were born, Grandfather took a one-way airline ticket to New York City and abandoned the family.

At the age of seven, Manolín, as he was nicknamed by family and friends, was forced to drop out of school to help sustain and support the family. He was the oldest boy, and his mother needed help. The boy sold his mother's candy sweets in the morning and worked as a delivery boy in the local town bakery in the afternoon. When he turned ten, grandmother asked her brother in Naguabo, Puerto Rico, to help her take care of the growing and unsettling boy. There was no other alternative, so he reluctantly agreed to stay with him.

The young boy spent seven years living with his uncle in the hills of a small town, east of San Juan, Naguabo, Puerto Rico. Many of Naguabo's rural neighborhoods are kilometers high in the mountains. His uncle lived in *El Cerro del Cabro* (The Goat Hill). In Puerto Rico, many rural neighborhoods were named after an animal, a person or another thing of significance to the inhabitants of the area. It was named like that because the mountain was full of goats. They were harmless creatures, but they were so many that their presence was unavoidable. It was impossible to walk up *El Cerro del Cabro* and not run into a goat.

The boy was forced to work from dawn to sunset. Every morning he walked two miles to get to his uncle's farm to milk the cows and pick up fresh eggs from a couple of hundred hens. Then he ran another three miles to make it to school on time. But he was just another mouth to feed, and every time he ran into mischief, he was physically and emotionally abused. One hot humid tropical night, his uncle came home drunk and looking for the boy:

"*¿Dónde está Manolín?*" (Where is Manolín?) my father's uncle asked.

"*Por ahí jugando, tío.*" (I am here uncle, playing.) answered my father who had just arrived from a friend's house.

"*¡Mira muchachito, ven acá¡*" (Look here, you little brat.) yelled the drunkard...

"No tío, no me des." (Please uncle, don't hit me.) screamed my father at the sight of his uncle charging toward him with an old heavy broomstick. It was too late. He had already been hit over the head several times with a heavy and wiry broomstick. There was a stream of blood coming down his forehead, and he ran for his life. The blood looked like a river running out of its course, finding its place to the sea. The boy ran away and slept outside that night. It was not the first or last time he was the victim of his uncle's rage. He came back the next day and stayed out of sight from his uncle for months.

Life was extremely difficult in Puerto Rico for my grandmother, and she gave up custody of her children. Three days before his seventeenth birthday, he celebrated with joy when he received a one-way airline ticket to New York City. He was tired of being enslaved by his uncle and thought things would be a lot better for him in New York City.

It was a cold winter night when the noisy plane reached the New York airport. Because of turbulence on the flight on the way down to New York, the flight was disturbingly rocky. The thousands of flashing lights Manolin saw from inside the plane startled him. When the plane hit the runway, it bobbled up and down until the tires settled on the unwelcoming airport. As he walked down the stairs outside the plane, the stark wind felt like it could cut his skin. He had an old torn sweater, and he felt the icy wind piercing every bone of his body. His lips began peeling, his ear felt like solid rock, and his knees trembled like an earthquake.

His father arrived two hours late, and Manolín walked up and down the airport until he noticed the figure of his old man getting out of the old Chevy. He had a black hat and wore a black coat, but Manolin immediately recognized his father. He was anxious to see him. It had been seven years since he last heard his voice. He could hear his heart beating like a drum. While other passengers received warm welcomes by relatives and friends, Manolin's father merely shook his son's hand, picked up his luggage and told him to get in the car.

The old man lived in East Harlem, also known as Spanish Harlem. The new Puerto Rican immigrants founded a Puerto Rico of their own called *El Barrio*. It stretched across 96th Street North to 127th Street and Fifth Avenue East in Manhattan. He lived on East 98th Street. Many of the late nineteenth century immigrants were moving into Long Island and other upstate neighborhoods, and the Puerto Ricans could find empty apartments in the old, abandoned lots.

Grandfather's apartment was on a third-floor tenement building. He had a three-room flat. The rooms were all lined up across each other. It had three bedrooms, a kitchen, living room and a bathroom. There was no space in his brother's bedroom, so Manolín slept on an old sofa in the living room. There was a fire escape in the kitchen. It was like living in a sardine can. During the long and cold winter nights, the heater hardly kept him warm. His father fought with the landlord for more heat, but the landlord shouted back and suggested they wear coats and sweaters inside the apartment to keep warm.

During the summers, El Barrio came alive with the sounds of *La Isla del Encanto* (Puerto Rico's nickname). Puerto Ricans brought their music, food and traditions with them to New York. The breath-taking smell of rice and beans, *arroz con gandures*, *sancocho* and *frituras (traditional Puerto Rican foods)* filled the air, and the sounds of Tito Rodríguez, Machito and a young mambo king, by the name of Tito Puente were common fixtures in

El Barrio. Puerto Rican flags were displayed on balconies, cars and window apartments. Men played dominoes outside, and women gathered in apartments to talk, gossip, and share family life experiences. For some inexplicable reason, Manolín thought he was still living in Puerto Rico.

Once in New York, he learned his father had sent for him so he could help feed the family. It was the very first day in New York, and he started to work in his father's bodega. Puerto Ricans worked in the tobacco industry, factories, hotels, city jobs, and a few owned small grocery stores known as bodegas. It was small, uncomfortable and had two narrow aisles filled with products from Puerto Rico. The old man had a connection at a post office in Puerto Rico, and for a small fee, a post office clerk would send him boxes of Goya beans and Bustelo coffee. Manolín was making a living for himself, but it meant hard work and sacrifice. His setting changed, but he still felt enslaved.

The young man spent evenings roaming around the neighborhood. He wondered why neighborhoods seemed to have boundaries. The Italians were jammed up in Hell's Kitchen and African Americans lived in Harlem, and the Irish were in a place called The Hill. It was practically impossible to get out of the neighborhood. If you crossed those boundaries, you had problems. Italians didn't want Puerto Ricans to walk into Third Avenue, and African-Americans did not allow them into Fifth Avenue. There were street gangs everywhere. Puerto Ricans arrived all at once, and in different colors making it more difficult for other ethnic groups to accept them. They came in black, brown, light brown, light-skin, olive-skin, white and a whole variety of skin colors and textures. For Puerto Ricans to befriend, talk and relate to people from other ethnic groups was something that they did every day in

Puerto Rico but in the United States people were very much aware of their ethnicity. This got a lot of Puerto Ricans in trouble, and gangs from other ethnicities were vigilant when a Boricua crossed the line.

Manolín learned some quick, painful lessons about prejudice. One day he roamed too much out of the geographical street limits and found himself lost in the middle of Hell's Kitchen. A policeman with a strong Italian accent stopped his car and yelled at him with an accusing tone.

"Hey, you, what you doing in this neighborhood?"

"Aim sorry. Aim lost" said my father in broken Puerto Rican English, fearing the worst.

"Turn around and get the hell out of here, we don't want any spics invading the community. Let this be the first and last time I catch you round here. Now, walk up two blocks, turn right and you back where you belong."

"Sank you" said my father with a sigh of relief and ran back to *El Barrio*. He had never run faster in his life.

After his eighteenth birthday, he decided to take his future in his hands. Thanks to a friend, he heard of the General Motor's automotive training program in Tarrytown, New York. It was his obsession to get out of *El Barrio*, and he saw Tarrytown as a place to begin a new one in Westchester County, New York. He registered in the program without the old man's approval. He knew his father needed him, and his father practically disowned him when he gave him the news, but Manolín packed his few belongings and took a train to Tarrytown. He wanted to build his own future, and this was that opportunity.

Carmen Gloria Carmona, my mother, came to New York in the early 50's too. Carmen's mother, Carmelita, gave birth to fifteen

14

children, but the first three died of malnutrition. After the first three died, then came Pepe, Isabel and my mother, Carmen. The 1930's were difficult economic times for Puerto Rico. The Island's economy was mainly dependent on the production of sugar cane and coffee. The sugar industry left workers unemployed during periods in between harvests, and there was a lot of competition from Hawaii and other Caribbean islands. Workers became unemployed for periods up to six months during the year (unemployment period between the harvest), and American farmers announced their packages to the unskilled and uneducated Puerto Rican worker. Thousands were forced to migrate to the United States.

Grandpa Alfredo was an alcoholic and a womanizer. He had a hell of a reputation. My grandmother wanted babies, so she got fifteen of them. By the time Carmelita gave birth to her fifteenth child, he had already moved in with a younger woman. The first three kids died of malnutrition. Carmelita brought up twelve kids alone. She did not have any means to support herself, but her strength of character and faith in God helped her through extreme poverty. She ironed clothes for neighbors and baked pastries to make ends meet.

Carmelita lived close to the beach, so the sea provided the family sustenance. The first born, Pepe went fishing to help feed the family. Even as a twelve-year-old boy, Pepe was a living legend. There was a lot of talk about his ability to catch crabs. He could catch more than forty dozen of them in one day. Carmelita saw her young son's talent as a blessing sent from God. When there was nothing on the family plate for his younger brothers and sisters, Pepe would leap out of his seat and run to the seacoast; an hour later, he would come back with a dozen crabs for supper.

Isabel and Carmen helped with the caring and feeding of the younger children. My grandparent's troubled marriage influenced the up bringing of the children. Carmen fell in love at sixteen, but Carmelita did not approve of her older boyfriend. Isabel married, but grandmother did not attend her wedding. There were striking physical similarities between Pablo, Isabel's husband, and Grandfather Alfredo, and grandmother did not want to be reminded of her disastrous relationship. Isabel moved to New York with her husband, and Carmen dropped out of high school and escaped to New York as well.

Carmen was uneasy with the turbulence during the flight to New York. A passenger sitting next to her got drunk and started talking about a possible airplane accident. She quietly and nervously started praying but felt relieved when the plane landed. It was a bitter cool January day when her plane arrived at the New York airport. She was strikingly beautiful, and a couple of airport workers could not take their eyes off the newly arrived *Boricua* (word for Puerto Rican with proud and dignified connotations). Her olive skin glowed at the touch of the caressing wind. Isabel arrived late, and Carmen almost took the next plane back to Puerto Rico.

Manuel and Carmen just happened to attend the same *Pentecostal* church in Brooklyn. Manolín set his eyes on the newly arrived *Boricua*, and it was love at first sight. It was a distant courtship. My father lived and worked in Tarrytown during the week and stayed over his brother's apartment in Brooklyn during the weekends to see Carmen and go to church. Seeing each other during the weekends was not exactly what my mother had in mind for a formal relationship. My father was persistent, and they married in April of 1962. By then, he was working full time at

General Motors in Tarrytown. They decided that Tarrytown was the ideal place to begin a new life.

I was born in Tarrytown, New York, in 1963. I was named after my father. I was never called Manuel though. For my parents and friends, I was simply called Junior. Manolín always wanted and prayed for a son, and the Lord granted his petition. Tarrytown is small but rich in history and pride. It is known for the setting of Washington Irving's legendary Sleepy Hollow and Rip Van Winkle. Tarrytown's junior high school bore the name of the influential American writer, and its high school was named after the legendary headless horseman.

Ever since General Motors opened a plant right on the edge of the Hudson River, it became a haven for newly arrived immigrants from all over the world. I can still picture the leaves turning colors in the fall, the flowers lighting up the schoolyard in spring, the snow covering Asbury Park like a blanket in winter, and the sun shining through the trees while I bathed in the swimming pool during the summer.

We could not afford a house. Mostly all *Latinos* lived in the project buildings. We lived at 126 Sally Street, apartment #6E. In the projects, dad paid a monthly rent according to his salary. When he worked overtime, the property manager increased the rent. Every time he worked an extra hour at work he waited until the office was closed to come back home. Management had a "joker" who was hired to spy on tenants, especially, when they took on part-time jobs. For some inexplicable reason, as a child I knew when the joker had informed administration about my dad's extra work.

My mother felt comfortable and at home there. Taking the elevator up to the sixth floor was a homecoming experience for

Carmen. The Puerto Rican sounds, and fresh smell of rice and beans were everyday wonders in the building. When we wanted *frijoles negros* (black beans), we visited the Domínguez' family in apartment #3A, and music was the specialty at the Sarmientos' apartment in #4C. When there was a birthday party, we all celebrated together. When someone was looking for a job, we all helped to find one. When there was tragedy, we all mourned together. It was a warm circle of friends who lived, celebrated, and cried together.

It was a small two-bedroom apartment. There was a small park in front of the building in which I played all day. My mother's undivided devotion lasted one year and four months. Elbita was born in July of 1964. My whole world came tumbling down. She was quite a beautiful baby girl, and her adoring cheeks and restless giggle enchanted my parents.

Our apartment came alive with family visits from Puerto Rico and New York City. My cousins, aunts and uncles coming home for the holidays provided truly wonderful moments. We sang songs and ate food from the Island. All but one of my mom's sisters moved to New York City.

I spoke English at school, but Spanish was the primary language in my house and at church. I lived in a household where two cultures and languages became one. There was no fuss or discussion about when to use English or Spanish. It was natural for me to speak English with my friends and Spanish with my family. I was just another typical American boy who spoke in two languages.

My neighbors were mostly African Americans. Our next-door neighbor was the assistant pastor of the church, which we attended. Ariel and Jenny were not only our best friends, but they were also my babysitters. Ariel, Jenny, and their children, Susie, Richie, and Shirley were like family to us. My parents belonged to the only Spanish-speaking church in town, Rock of Salvation. There I learned about God and developed an acute interest in the Bible and its foundations. There were kids from Cuba, Ecuador, Colombia, and Puerto Rico. We worshipped, played, and had good times together. We identified with each other.

The pastor, Louie Rios, was like a second father to me. He had a son about my age, and Luisito and I became close friends. Many of my weekends were spent at the pastor's house. In one of my fondest memories, I remember riding with the pastor as a toddler to pick up people to go to church. He used to test my resistance by squeezing my knee with his strong hands. I resisted as much as I could but always ended up laughing my heart out. I loved Pastor Louie as we called him and learned to love God through him. We had the utmost respect for Pastor Louie. Even as a young toddler, I tried my best not to sleep during Sunday sermons.

I belonged to the Royal Rangers at church, and we spent one week during the summers hiking and camping out at Bear Mountain. The Royal Rangers were like Christian boy scouts, and their values complemented the ones received at home. We had softball tournaments during the summer and played football games with American churches in the winter. There were seasonal garage sales. Something was always going on at church. Those years are like a beautiful dream that you have and do not want to let go of when you wake up in the morning.

Father's jobs prevented him from sharing more time with us, but he always took time to take us to a park or a local town fair. We also drove to the city every so often and visited relatives. One of the most memorable drives to the city was on the morning of

January 1, 1973. It was about 11:00 am, and we were minutes away from Yankee Stadium when we heard the tragic news on the radio. Roberto Clemente's airplane had disappeared along the Atlantic coast while on a flight to aid the victims of the Nicaragua earthquake.

Mother was dedicated and caring. She was the typical mother woman. Every now and then, she took up a part time job at Woolworth's but once the building administrator heard my mom was working, he would increase the rent. I remember overhearing one of the conversations between my parents where they argued about whether my mom should continue working or not.

"Ma, I'm sorry, but you gotta quit your job."

"What... we need the extra money!"

"I'm sorry, sweetheart. The administrator says we're going to have to pay more rent." I did not want to hear anymore.

She spent a lot of time playing dominoes and cards with other women from church. Carmen and her best friends, Jenny and Aida, were always doing something together. All three were bringing up children and taking care of the family. They shared stories, frustrations and experiences that they had as wives and mothers. David, Luisito and I were busy playing and running into innocent mischief. These were the best of times.

As a child, I never felt different from other boys. I grew up like any other American boy. I loved television and watched Superman and Batman and learned the Pledge of Allegiance by heart. Even as a boy, I felt great pride in being an American. The July 4th parades and fireworks along the Hudson are powerful flashbacks engraved in my soul.

My pre-kindergarten teacher was physically impressive. Mrs. Dye was a six foot five-inch-tall African American woman that scared the daylights out of you by saying "hello". Her immense body frame and huge hands enhanced my impression of her. It was my first school experience, and it was one that I would never forget. I learned to deeply love and respect Mrs. Dye. She was dedicated, hard-working and caring. She lighted up the classroom with a smile, and her words were like music to your soul. I learned the alphabet, but the love she gave me complemented my mother's daily guidance and affection. That is why the time I spent with her was meaningful and has stayed in my conscious forever.

Then came kindergarten. When I was five, I was about as normal as any other boy my age. For reasons still unknown, my playground buddies started calling me Little Junior. I was not little, but I sure did feel that way. I was bullied and found myself running home every day. There was a gang at school that wanted to beat me up, and I broke a new world record every day. This continued through first and second grades. During the summer, in between second and third grades, I grew five to six inches. Instead of calling me, Little Junior, now I was plain Junior. The kids that ran after me were now shorter than me.

As a child, I was nostalgic for Puerto Rico. I grew up with the colors, stories and sounds of *La Isla* (island of Puerto Rico). My mother did a lot of singing in Spanish while she sewed socks and made dresses for my sisters. Among her favorites were *En Mi Viejo San Juan* by Noel Estrada and *Lamento Borincano* by Rafael Hernández (Puerto Rican classic songs). Every time she sang these songs, tears would roll down her rosy cheek. I'd often ask her why she was crying, but I never got an answer. My parents spoke about going back to their homeland. My mother showed me pictures of my young uncles, Diego and Eli. She called her mother at least once a month, and I sometimes spoke with her too. My grandmother always spoke about her garden. The flowers were bright yellow, and roses came in red, purple and wine. Every time my mother spoke about the garden, I imagined a beautiful rainbow of colors. There was also a lot of talk about the *coquí*, a small Puerto Rican toad which could not be found anywhere in the world. I could sometimes hear the *coquí*, *coquí* sound on the telephone receiver. The *coquí* is named after the sound it makes. Whenever I thought of my parent's homeland, I heard the repetitious, happy and musical sound*, coquí, coquí, coquí.*

I had never been to Puerto Rico, but it lived in me. As a young boy, I had a lot of freedom. My mother had a hard time getting me away from the playground in front of our building. I would let her scream my name at least ten times before responding. I played baseball on a little league team from our town. My coach, Mr. Kelly, wanted me to be the next Roberto Clemente. The New York Mets had just won the 1969 World Series, and it seemed like everybody was a Mets fan. To top the World Series, my sister Lilly was born during the playoffs of 1969.

In the fourth grade, I became very popular among my classmates. I was also a straight A student and developed a superiority complex. I had a crush on my English teacher. I loved listening when she read Huckleberry Finn and Tom Sawyer. Mrs. Mc Grath was very proud of her parent's homeland. She often spoke about going back to her parent's homeland, Ireland. She described its green pastures and plain valleys and even showed off an Irish Flag on top of her desk. One day, she asked us what we wanted to be when we grew up.

"Manuel, how about you?" asked Mrs. Mc Grath with her sweet and soft delicate voice.

"I wanna be a writer!" I quickly replied.

"A writer, Manuel?" asked Mrs. Mc Grath with a sudden change of tone in her voice.

"That's right, Mrs. Mc Grath" I answered with pride and dignity.

"Why not play baseball or soccer, Manuel?"

"I wanna be a writer!"

"Well, good luck then!"

I was outstanding in sports and was the tallest boy in the classroom. On my tenth birthday, my father bought me my first bicycle. It was navy blue with white wall tires. I loved that bike. After falling down many times, I taught myself how to ride it. The bike made me feel powerful, free and distinguished. There was something about the bike that made me feel on top of the world.

I began a puppy love relationship with a girl from school. Karen was as tall as I was and had dark hair right up to her shoulders and dark brown eyes. She wore a brown coat with a white furry collar in winter. Her lips were round and lively. She had the cutest smile, which accentuated her beautiful face. I walked her home and carried her books from school. Karen's family lived in a huge house on the other side of town. We played outside, but I was never invited inside the house. Her father, Mr. Robert Roth, was one of the richest men in Tarrytown. Once he asked me where I lived, and I saw his face turn red when I proudly mentioned the Tarrytown public projects. He was also an honorable member of the Tarrytown City Council.

Karen liked sports; so we played football together. We sat down in the lunchroom together. I felt good around her. Our friendship grew stronger through the fifth grade. It was during the summer of 1974 that Karen and I reached puberty. She had blossomed into a beautiful young brunette. I was the tallest in my homeroom and my shoulders were the widest in school.

At the beginning of the sixth grade, an event occurred that has influenced my way of thinking since. I was excited when I saw Karen, but I immediately noticed her indifference. I approached her, but she seemed cold and nervous. The sparkling eyes were gone. Her eternal smile had faded into the sunset. I tried talking to her, but she was not listening to me.

"Karen, can I talk to you?"

She stayed quiet, and moments later she replied.

"The problem is that you and I can't be friends anymore" she said looking the other way.

"What are you talking about?" I asked.

"Well, Jews and Puerto Ricans are people of different races."

"Hey... what do you mean? Who cares?"

"I'm Jewish and you're a Puerto Rican."

"So what... we're Americans!"

"You and I can never marry."

"Marry... I don't understand. What are you talking about?"

"Leave me alone" she said and ran up the stairs.

No further explanations were made. I did not understand her. I knew that my parents were Puerto Rican, but I never thought that was important. I couldn't sleep for days. For the first time in my life, I realized there were differences between people that went beyond my boyhood imagination. Karen never spoke to me again. It took me years to understand her words and actions. My parents had brought me up aware of my heritage, but I never thought it meant anything important in terms of having friends from different nationalities. I was wrong. She made me aware that I was different.

I was a Puerto Rican. How? …Why? The years and experiences would shed light on my confusion.

GROWING UP IN TWO WORLDS

In 1974, the year of the Watergate scandal, my parents moved back to their homeland, Puerto Rico. Mrs. McGrath had frequently mentioned a homeland, but I never really understood what she meant. The people at church gave us a nice farewell party. There was a lot of food and laughter, but I was sad and angry with my parent's decision. My life in Tarrytown was ending abruptly, and I felt confused and weary. It didn't make sense. Puerto Rico for me was letters, pictures, and postcards. It was a fantasy island. I said goodbye to Luisito, Freddie, Juanito, David and Nephtali. Karen didn't even seem to care when Mrs. Russo, my homeroom teacher, announced that I was moving to Puerto Rico.

I had been to Puerto Rico several times on vacation, but this was a permanent move. From my mother's mood, I knew she was not happy about moving to the so-called Island of Enchantment, but father stressed that a marriage meant personal sacrifices from time to time. I confronted her a few days before we moved to Puerto Rico.

"Ma, do we have to move?"

My mother took a few seconds to answer the question.

"Well, your father thinks it's the best thing for us."

"I don't wanna go to Puerto Rico."

"Who are you going to stay with?"

"I can stay with *Titi*."

"*Titi* lives in the city."

"Come on, mami, I wanna stay. How about my friends?"

"Nonsense. Your father will not allow it!"

Having just finished her statement, she stood up and locked herself up in her bedroom. My mother had a fourth child, Cindy, and she had constant mood swings. When the time arrived, father and Elbita went first, and Mom, Cindy, Lilly and I waited for about a month until he found a job and an apartment.

It was a cold gray autumn afternoon when our next-door neighbors, Ariel and Jenny, drove us to the airport. The leaves fell off the trees faster than usual. We drove away from my birthplace. Everything seemed to be moving in slow motion. I did not want to miss any details of the town I grew up in. I looked at the old lot where my dad had flown the first kite with me several years before. I asked Ariel to drive by the school. I did not blink my eyes when we slowly drove by Winfield L. Morse Elementary School. My heart sank when we cruised through the Tappan Zee Bridge. I looked back and saw father's ex-working place, General Motors. It was a magnificent sight. The plant was on the bank of the river. From a distance, it looked like a postcard, picture-perfect.

Father quit his dream job after fifteen years of hard work and disappointments. He sometimes worked three shifts, and his health had deteriorated. Because of his asthma, the doctor recommended a warmer climate. He suggested that his homeland, a tropical paradise, was the ideal place for his health. It was just the right excuse, in my opinion.

I was quiet and thoughtful during the endless drive to the airport. Mother kept pretty much to herself during the hour-long drive to John F. Kennedy International Airport. My sisters, Lilly and Cindy, made mother's life miserable by crying and complaining along the way. Lillian was four years and Cindy was a newborn, and they could care less about moving to Puerto Rico, but I was a pre-adolescent and was leaving so many friends behind.

Home. I was going to the Island of Puerto Rico: home of the sugar cane and banana fruit, home of the tall skyscraper trees and the mirror blue green sea. These were the images that I had from the pictures sent back with father and Elba eating a long piece of wood called sugar cane. There were other pictures of father and sister on the beach. They looked happy.

The plane ride to Puerto Rico was rough and bumpy. My baby sister cried all through the flight. Mother complained about the heat on the plane. I observed her pain in silence. Right after the plane landed in Puerto Rico, Cindy vomited all over mother's new dress. I looked the other way.

I remember getting off the plane in Isla Verde, Puerto Rico. It was a hot and sticky afternoon. The sun felt like fire on my skin. The temperature was ninety-eight degrees and climbing. I tried cheering myself up by thinking I was home, but I was insecure of what the future had in store for me. My father and sister Elbita came to pick us up at the airport. They were jubilant to see the rest of the family.

We moved into a second-story wood apartment in a rural barrio of Luquillo, a small beach town fifteen miles from the capital of Puerto Rico, San Juan. I finally had my own room, but it was full of mosquitoes and bugs. We had to use mosquito nets on top of our beds so that the flies would not attack us during the night. You could hear the zooming of the mosquitoes trying to land on your flesh. The nights in Puerto Rico were hot and humid, and it rained every day.

Our landlord enjoyed turning the water off every afternoon. While our neighbors had water, we didn't have enough for a shower. My father was hired as a mechanic by National Car Rental at the airport. The money was not enough to support us, so he took a part-time job during the evenings and another part-time job as a mechanic during the weekends. Mother complained that the money coming in was not enough and applied for food stamps. Things were so rough and difficult that I had to sell my trumpet so that my sisters and I could wear clothes to school.

At the age of twelve, I spent the summer working in construction. My uncle was the contractor and hired me as a helper. I did everything from mixing cement with sand to making concrete and carrying 100-pound sandbags. Tio Pedro cursed at me every time he gave me instructions, and I felt like quitting every time he did so, but my family needed the money. The money earned was to buy clothes for the upcoming school year. Father ended up working harder than he had ever worked in his life. It was painful to watch him come in late at night from work and leave before sunrise. He lived tired. It was a painstaking time.

Mother registered me in the local public school. It was a five-room building in a rural barrio called Juan Martin. There was no gym. Students had to wear uniforms, and teachers could use corporal punishment. Even the name of the school sounded weird to me, Carolina G. De Veve. On the first day of school, my sixth-grade teacher, Mrs. Tapia, asked me, *¿Cuál es tu segundo apellido?* I was dumbfounded. You see, in the United States, my mother's last name was never needed, mentioned, or asked for in school. In Puerto Rico, a second last name was a must. But Mrs. Tapia asked who my mother was and immediately knew that it was Carmona. I hated it. I had nothing against my mother's last name, but it was new for me, and I didn't like the sound of it. For me, Carmona was half a car and half *mona* (female monkey).

To add insult to injury, and from that moment on, she always called me Carmona and so did the rest of the teachers in that school. It just so happened that all my eight aunts and four uncles had studied in Carolina G. De Veve elementary school, too, and I was the oldest grandson and the new Carmona in town. My classmates called me *Gringo* and *Nuyorican*. These were new terms for me. I didn't have a clue what those words meant, but they laughed and giggled when they called me like that. Someone told me that Gringo was because I had moved from the United States, and Nuyorican was supposed to mean that I was half Puerto Rican and half New York Rican or something like that. I hated those names, too, but there were too many Boricuas to fight.

Who was I? What was I? Where was I? My confusion grew worse with the further development of puberty. I was five feet, eight inches tall and twelve years old, and my body was developing fast. My father was too busy working, so I learned about the facts of life through my new-found friends. Instead of father talking to me about the birds and the bees, my new Puerto Rican buddies gave me a lesson or two on sex. They helped open my eyes to the world.

My homeroom teacher, Mrs. Tapia, told me that she would test my abilities to read in Spanish. If I failed, she would place me in a lower grade. The evaluation was done exclusively on a reading of a paragraph in Spanish. Thanks to my education at home and church, my Spanish was even better than those who had been in Puerto Rico all their lives, and I was allowed to stay in the sixth grade. I still don't understand how, but I adjusted rapidly and made friends fast. For wanting to compete and get good grades, I was nicknamed *soberbia* (overtly proud). For speaking English, I was ridiculed and made fun of, so I decided to hide my English. Although I spoke Spanish well, classmates laughed out loud, so I kept quiet. Despite all that, I graduated with honors from the sixth-grade graduation.

I entered junior high school feeling like a hero. My hormones were running wild. I was twelve, but I was almost five feet nine inches tall. The girls in high school showed interest in me. Suddenly, I felt unique and special. Seventh grade was my worst academic year ever, and I was almost left back. My temper grew along my body, and I became a bully. I fought constantly, and teachers took me to the office every day. I barely passed the seventh grade.

My family moved from Luquillo to Río Grande, a town just a few miles from Luquillo. Father worked for the Agricultural Department as a diesel mechanic. The Agricultural Department provided him with a house and a pick-up truck to take home. Elbita and I were adolescents, Lilly and Cindy were running around the house, and my mother tried to keep us well fed and in good health.

Mother went back to school to finish high school and graduated in 1978. She was accepted as a part-time student at Puerto Rico Junior College in San Juan. I admired her efforts. She was part of a unique academic program where students took classes at home through their television sets. When she sat down in front of the television with a notebook, books and a pen, I often made fun of her. Every three weeks, I accompanied her to San Juan to take her unit exams at the home campus in San Juan.

We called the house in Río Grande, "*La colina*," because it was way up in the hill and stood all by itself in a two-acre property. It was a lonely house, and I spent endless hours yearning for New

York. I remember watching the 1979 NCAA championship between Indiana and Michigan State from "La colina," A couple of basketball players, Magic Johnson and Larry Bird, were playing the college game of a lifetime. Magic's team won, but Larry and Magic would meet a few more times before the 1980 s were over. I used to drive my father crazy by singing "Bye Bye, Miss American Pie" every night. I never went to sleep before listening to the Star Spangled Banner and "*La Borinqueña*" (Puerto Rican national anthem) on television. I lived in Puerto Rico but dreamed constantly of going back to New York City.

In the meantime, a new school turned me into a shy person. It was difficult for me to make new friends. There was a new system in school called *quinmestres* where students could take as many credits as possible and pass to another grade ahead of time. I saw it as an opportunity to get ahead in school and have more vacation time. Plus, there was also the possibility of going back to New York. I completed my junior high school credits in March of 1978, two months ahead of time. I secretly wrote a letter to Aunt Isabel in New York, and she sent me a one-way airline ticket.

When the day arrived for me to go to New York, mother locked herself up in her room. I said goodbye but only heard her sobbing. It was raining like mad when my father took me to the airport at Isla Verde. After four years, I was going back to New York. Father was dead silent during the drive to the airport. I was fifteen years old and was leaving my family for the first time in my life. When my father hugged me before I entered the plane, my heart was broken and shattered, but I held back the tears.

THE UMBRELLA FACTORY

It was a dark and gloomy night when the plane landed at John F. Kennedy International Airport in New York at twelve midnight. I momentarily saw flashes of a headless horseman, remembering the story, Sleepy Hollow, read to me as a sixth grader at Winfield L. Morse Elementary School. The story, staged in 1790 in the Dutch settlement of Tarrytown, New York, is about Ichabod Crane, a schoolmaster from Connecticut, who competes with Abraham "Brom Bones" Van Brunt for the hand of eighteen-year-old Katrina Van Tassel, daughter of a rich farmer. When Crane leaves a party at the Van Tassel home on an autumn night, he is followed by the so-called Headless Horseman, who is supposedly the ghost of a Hessian trooper who lost his head during a battle which took place during the American Revolutionary War. Crane disappears from town, leaving Katrina to marry Brom Bones.

The fasten seatbelt sign started to light on and off. The passenger sitting next to me had been drinking all through the flight and vomited when the pilot turned off the seat belt sign. The sudden stop turned his stomach upside down. The smell was like rotten garlic, and I nearly fainted. I barely escaped the disaster and quickly stood up and joined the dozens of people running down the aisle of the 727.

It was the first time that I was traveling alone, so I was somewhat anxious and nervous when I went to get my luggage at the baggage claim area. I immediately spotted my light blue suitcase, but a fellow passenger claimed it belonged to him. We argued, but much to my dismay he ran off with it. Few minutes later he returned it and said that it was not his. An hour later, Aunt Isabel and a friend of hers arrived and drove us to Brooklyn. It seemed like a long drive to Brooklyn, and I was perplexed at the gray sight of the city. As I noticed hundreds of abandoned buildings and lots of garbage out on the city streets, I felt my heart burning and for a minute had visions of the Island beaches. When we got out of the car, I observed a couple of drunkards sleeping on the steps that lead up and into my aunt's apartment.

She lived in a small two-bedroom apartment on Huron Street, Brooklyn. It was a Polish-neighborhood full of old and ancient houses. You could hear the house squeak as you walked up the stairs. Her apartment was on a block of three-story buildings. All the houses were exactly alike and only the colors distinguished each one. Her apartment was a two-room second floor walk-up. Nothing about it was particularly interesting except for the fact that all the rooms were connected to each other. If my aunt wanted to go to the bathroom, she had to walk pass my bedroom. The very first night, I was introduced to the world of cockroaches. I woke up at about three o'clock in the morning to go to the bathroom, and I was in shock when I turned on the lights, thousands of cockroaches had invaded the kitchen. I let out a scream.

"*Titi*, why so many cockroaches in the kitchen?"

My aunt put on a sleeping robe and came to my rescue.

"*Muchacho*, go back to bed. They were here before Christopher Columbus discovered America," my aunt replied.

After a while, I got used to cockroaches. Every time I felt them on my back, I shivered all over, and the cockroaches flew across

34

the bedroom. It was as if they owned the apartment airspace. Other creatures also visited me every now and then during the night. Big fat rats seemed to enjoy a roller coaster ride on my butt every so often, so I got used to that too. I learned to adapt quickly.

The very next day my aunt told me I had to get a job. I thought I was going to have a week to settle down. I was fifteen years old, but I looked older. I was already six feet tall and weighed about one hundred and ninety-five pounds. Aunt Nerida came by at six in the morning, but I was still sleeping. They woke me up by pouring a cold glass of water over my head. A steady drop went right into my ear, and I woke up quickly.

She took me to about forty factories, but there were no jobs anywhere. I went home a little depressed, and my aunts calmed me down by assuring me that I would find a job the next day. The next day I woke up at five-thirty a.m. and was ready by the time Aunt Nerida knocked on the door. At the very first factory, we were told that there was a position available. The foreman wanted proof of age, so I went home and falsified my birth certificate. I was hired and started working the next day.

It was an umbrella factory. The smell of cigars and tobacco filled the air. There was so much smoke, that there was a thick layer like a cloud floating in the air. It was not unusual to mistakenly bump into people while one walked to the bathroom. The constant tic-tack of a hammer hitting the umbrella together with a lath was sound heard every second.

The factory workers came in different colors and nationalities. Puerto Ricans, Dominicans, Cubans, Poles, and Italians were just a few of the nationalities found in the factory. It was like the United Nations had sent a select group of working-class characters to represent them at the umbrella factory. I was making $2.63 an hour; not bad for a fifteen-year-old. I took home about $80.00, and after giving my aunt $20.00 and sending my mom $20.00, I was left with $40.00, which I spent at Mc Donald's and on train tokens.

My buddies at work were all hooked on something. Quique was always sniffing cocaine and rush. Quique was crazy, and he talked about hanging out in *El Barrio* in Manhattan. He said Friday nights there were filled with artists called poets who read poetry and combined it with music. I thought it was cool, but I remembered my aunt's warnings about *El Barrio*, so I always brushed him off. He wanted me to go with him to the Lower East Side. He insisted that I needed to know what street life was all about. Quique seemed like a nice guy, but his drug use was destroying him. One day he sniffed rush so hard, he was knocked unconscious for five minutes. Pedro smoked marihuana and ate cocaine for breakfast. His teeth were white as snow, and his breath smelled of wet grass after a spring shower. I started to feel comfortable with the smell of marihuana. I worked right in between Quique and Pedro, so I got hooked on the smell. There wasn't a day that I was not offered drugs, but I never accepted the offer. Pedro called me a preacher, but I laughed and turned him down again. My aunt thought I was hooked on drugs, but the truth is I never accepted Pedro's nor Quique's offers.

The factory women also noticed the new kid on the block, but I did not give into their sexual innuendoes. The working area had Penthouse and Playboy centerfolds of the month taped all over the wall. The first few days I stared gracefully but after a few days I didn't even notice the beautiful babes on the factory wall.

Isabel went to a small church around the corner, and I went, too. It was a small Pentecostal church with about twenty members. The pastor spoke about the coming of Jesus and the end of the world in every sermon. Reverend Caratinni was an easy going, outspoken and loud-speaking pastor. He was five feet, three inches tall and weighed close to three hundred pounds. He was bald and had a bright spot that shined right on the top of his head. Reverend Caratinni screamed and yelled from the altar, and his hair flew up and down with every swing of his words. He had my aunt crazy with the coming of Christ, but I had too much on my mind to worry about the end of the world. Going to church was always important for me, but Caratinni exaggerated every word. They had nine services a week, one each weekday, including Saturdays, and three on Sundays. I sometimes went five and six times a week. Out of respect to my aunt, I visited quite frequently but when there were three services on a Sunday, I would negotiate two with my aunt. It was too much church for a fifteen-year-old.

I spent my weekends visiting my aunts. On a blazing hot New York Saturday afternoon, I was visiting Aunt Barbarita and smoke started coming into the apartment. In a matter of seconds, fire burst all over. I tried saving the new camcorder, but the smoke in the bedroom was suffocating. When I tried getting close to the camcorder, I saw shades of black smoke sprinting through my aunt's bedroom wall. I ran back to the living room while my cousins flew down the fire escape. I grabbed my aunt's Chihuahua and jumped down the stairs. The fire destroyed everything. We barely got out alive. The fire was like a wild horse in a rodeo. Its fury was devastating. The back draft almost killed two firemen. In less than five minutes, the apartment with all her belongings was gone.

My aunt lost everything. She cried her heart out. It was a desperate scene, but I could only watch in disbelief, because we barely got out alive. People from social services got her a new apartment, and brothers and sisters from church got her furniture and clothes. When we called our uncle, he asked for the safety of the Chihuahua.

Towards the end of my ordeal at the umbrella factory, I was carrying boxes of beach umbrellas into a truck, and a box slipped out of my hands and cut one of my fingers. I asked my Polish boss, Mr. Walinski, permission to wash out the blood from my hand.

"Hey, Mr. Walinski, can I wash my hands; I'm bleeding?"

"Sorry, Hernández, if you go to the bathroom, you're fired."

"Come on, can't you see I'm bleeding?" I implored.

"I don't care if you're bleeding or suffocating, just get those beach babies in the truck!" he said with bitterness in his eyes.

"What are you talking about?" I reacted.

"Hey, do you spic English?"

"Mr. Walinski?"

"That's right, bozo. You stay where you are, or you're fired."

I took five minutes to ponder those words. This was my moment of truth. What would I do? Was the umbrella factory going to be part of my future? Should I go back to school? These questions went back and forth in my mind while I wrapped up my hand in a co-worker's handkerchief. I promised myself that from there on I would change my attitude towards school; get good grades and study at the university.

A few weeks later, I was laid off from the umbrella factory. I had a few days off and decided to call my hometown buddies. I had been in New York City for two months, but I had not been able to visit Tarrytown. I was anxious to go back to the town of my upbringing.

On the following Saturday morning, I got up early, packed a backpack and ran towards the subway station. The Metro North train ran right across the Hudson River, and I anticipated what Tarrytown would look like.

At a slow then hurried pace, the train passed the city buildings and headed to Westchester County. I looked around the train car and saw a bunch of people, none of whom I recognized. To my left, there was an elderly couple that was sleeping. To my right, there was a young teenage couple passionately kissing. I peeked out the window and observed the tall and proud sailboats, and the brave and strong tugboats along the historic river. My heart ran rapidly when I got off at the old Tarrytown train station. The train station was on the other side of General Motors, so I spent a few moments looking at father's old working place. The cars were stacked up like giant pants hanging in a Laundromat. The plant where he had worked for fifteen years of his life to build a future for himself and his family was still standing strong. My buddies were running a bit late, so I gathered my stray of emotions. Willie and Marshall came around to pick me up. Marshall was one of the old bullies who had smacked my face as a young boy. I asked him if he remembered little Junior:

"Hey, you remember Little Junior…"

"No, I've never heard of the guy" he nervously answered.

"You sure, I'm Little Junior," I said defiantly.

"First time I ever see yaw…" he said while a big bead of sweat ran down his forehead.

"You look like a Marshall I knew a few years back."

I was a couple of years younger than Marshall, but I was taller and heavier than him. I dropped the subject because I didn't want to spoil the homecoming. It was him alright, but I had my revenge by seeing fear in his eyes while I questioned him.

Tarrytown had not changed much in four years. There was a Mc Donald's on the corner of Madison and Sampson Street, but I did not recognize other new businesses or buildings. The town was so small that I walked up and down the main streets in less than a half hour. I went to the old pizzeria, but it had changed owners, and the pizza was not as good as the old one. My old schools were still there, and I imagined how beautiful and attractive Karen would be by now. I asked Willie to drive around her house, but the house looked empty and hollow, and we continued our drive through the land of Rip Van Winkle and Sleepy Hollow.

In a matter of seconds, Willie was smoking pot and Marshall was sniffing white powder, which I later identified as cocaine. I was sitting in the back of the car. The year was 1978, and my buddies were pumping "It Feels So Good" by Chuck Mangione on the radio. Marshall asked if I wanted cocaine, and I said no. They laughed at my response, and I felt uncomfortable and uneasy about coming home. We went to see Felix, another of my neighborhood buddies, and he was selling and pushing drugs at the corner of Sally Street. All my buddies were using or pushing drugs. They offered me drugs again and again, I refused.

"Come on June, try some weed," said Felix with a sarcastic smile on his face.

"Na, that's not for me."

"Hey, Junior, you come here, and you don't do drugs with your old-time buddies" yelled Marshall.

The smoke in the car was like a dense cloud in your face and the pressure was building, and I was almost ready to give in. Instead of doing drugs, I bought a bottle of Bacardi and drank half of it to prove that I was part of the group. The very next morning, I hopped on the first train back to New York City.

I stayed in New York a few more weeks working in construction but when August came around, I was ready to go back to Puerto Rico. My aunt Isabel wanted me to stay, but I did not feel completely at home in New York. The pressure was coming from many fronts at the same time, and I preferred to escape instead of confronting it.

It was a smooth flight back home, early afternoon, so I got to see the light blue green sea and the daunting palm trees as the plane flew above the northern Island seashore. The landing was perfect, and the passengers applauded when the captain announced our arrival. I was told by a European couple sitting next to me that they had traveled all over the world and had never heard passengers applaud at a landing. I said it was an old Puerto Rican tradition, and they nodded in disbelief. The passengers were ecstatic with joy. I stayed quiet but shared their emotions.

My parents and sisters came to pick me up. I hugged them and was happy to be back home. I promised my mother that I was going to get good grades in high school and was going to study at the university. I was relieved when my father opened the door of the old Nova. I was thoughtful and quiet during the drive home.

MY BACHELOR'S DEGREE

I entered high school feeling like I was Napoleon Bonaparte and had come back a conqueror. Classes had begun two weeks earlier, so I had lots of school homework to make up. It was my first day of school, and I was already in trouble. My school buddies wanted to skip classes and go to the new mall in Carolina, Puerto Rico. I resisted temptation and stayed in school. Flashbacks of the umbrella factory and my experience in Tarrytown were fresh in my memory whenever I thought of quitting school and going wrong. Aunt Isabel had sent a letter where she included a note from my ex-boss from the Umbrella Factory. He wanted me back, but I remembered the insults and humiliation and politely declined the offer. I wanted to change my academic performance and go to college. That was my goal, and no one was going to stray me from it.

My years in high school were relatively quiet. I did not get involved in school clubs, and I was not distracted by girls and sports. I graduated with honors and was accepted at the University of Puerto Rico, Rio Piedras Campus. The University of Puerto Rico is the oldest and most prestigious academic institution on the Island. Only five percent of the high school students that applied were accepted, so it was an opportunity I had looked forward to ever since I entered high school.

I began my undergraduate studies at UPR in the fall of 1981. My father had just bought a new house in Fajardo, and he was working at the Navy Base at Roosevelt Roads in Ceiba. My mother was still completing her Bachelor of Arts degree and worked as an assistant teacher at the same time. She worked at school during the day and drove an hour to the university during the late afternoon. I worried about her driving home so late, but my mother's desire to finish her studies went beyond my comprehension. It was my mother's example that gave me the strength and courage to study at the University. Elba was finishing high school and Lilly and Cindy were in elementary school.

I received a warm welcome during my first week in school. It was during my second class on my first day at the university that a small group of students came into the Spanish class and interrupted the professor's lecture. They spoke about a student strike vote. The issue was tuition. Credits were increased from five to fifteen dollars. I did not understand the problem. It was so financially difficult for me to study in the first place. My father was getting started with his mortgage payments and making sacrifices so that I could study, and my mother was working and studying to get me through college. Students on strike interrupted classes, and the Chancellor suspended classes until negotiations with the striking students came to an end. The semester dragged through Christmas and finally ended in March of 1982.

Although I did well my first couple of years in college, I was not completely sure about what I wanted to study, and I continued to yearn for New York. I was a full-grown twenty-year-old Nuyorican and the call of the city was ingrained in my blood.

During the summer after my sophomore year, I went back to New York. I worked in construction and saved money to help with my studies. This time I stayed at Pastor Louie's house. My boyhood minister had a blessed and prosperous congregation in the Bronx. I was treated like a king at his house. Whenever the pastor walked down the aisle, we people in his church admired him. He knew the Bible by heart like John Milton and touched all with his words and wisdom. He provided me with a room, a job and food. Plus, there were more than a few cute girls at church that I could befriend and drive around in the Caddy. I found myself caught up between staying in New York City and going back to Puerto Rico. Pastor Louie asked me to stay, and the dilemma wrestled in my mind for more than a week. I did not want to let my mother down. She always came up in my thoughts whenever I thought of dropping out of college; her efforts to complete college education was the determining factor in my decision to go back to the Island.

Louie expressed his disappointment with my decision and asked his wife to take me to the airport. It was a silent drive along the Major Deegan Expressway. Mrs. Rios was a slow driver, so I got to look at the city once more. She dropped me off at the airport and quickly drove off. I carried my luggage and hurried to the gate. I had mixed feelings about going back to Puerto Rico. My soul and heart were divided. I was happy about going back to the Island but disillusioned about leaving the city.

I was back at UPR for my junior year. I decided to follow my mother's footsteps and become a teacher. I wasn't entirely sure about being a teacher, but I thought it was the right thing to do at the time. I observed classes at the university high school, and I was shocked when a fifteen-year-old girl sat on top of the teacher's desk with her legs crossed and showing her panties. My heart pounded heavily, my knees trembled, and I sweat profusely. Suddenly, I had my doubts about becoming the next teacher in the family. With two part-time jobs and six classes per semester, I completed my junior year. I still wasn't completely sure about becoming a teacher, but a professor at UPR, Prof. Helia Santana, motivated me. Prof. Santana encouraged me and got the best out of me when I performed in front of the class. She challenged me to be creative and original. Although I played with the idea of changing majors, Prof. Santana convinced me that I had what it took to be a teacher.

A year of making commitments and decisions left me with the idea of getting away from it all during the summer, and where else to go but to New York. This time I looked forward to a summer of fun and enjoyment. My father drove me to the airport and made the usual warnings, but my mind was already in The Big Apple.

It was a smooth flight to New York. For the first time I could remember, there was no turbulence at all. Just as we were beginning to descend at 30,000 feet, the captain interrupted an old episode from the TV series Happy Days and announced the following, "This is your captain, Lewis Graves, we will begin our descent to the greater New York area in a few minutes, but we ask you to wear your seatbelts along the way. We are experiencing technical difficulties with the landing gear and may need to make an emergency landing. We are taking all the necessary precautions and expect to land safely. We apologize for any inconveniences this may cause you. Thank you again and have a great stay in New York City, or wherever your destination may be."

There was a cold silence inside the plane. The passengers did not know how to react. The flight attendants started checking the oxygen masks, and I was filled with uncertainty and confusion. An old woman who sat next to the aisle made the sign of the cross. I looked the other way, and a passenger sitting next to the window was reading a big black Bible. My mind was empty, but I did not like the tone in Captain Graves' voice. I closed my eyes and prayed. I remembered Psalm 23 and repeated it several times. I remembered telling my sister once that I thought I would die before I turned twenty-one, but I was already in the prime of my life and with a future ahead of me.

After twenty-minutes, the New York City lights were visible, and I felt a little better. Once again, Captain Graves interrupted Happy Days, "Ladies and gentlemen, please put your heads down with your hands folded inside your lap. We expect to land safely but would appreciate your cooperation. Thank you and I will greet you at the door before you exit the plane." The old lady was mumbling a prayer, and the passenger with the big black Bible was holding it close to his heart. I spoke with God and asked Him to forgive my sins but feared the worst. The plane started losing altitude, and the captain jerked the landing gear. We were told to keep our heads down, and I heard a few "Ai Dios mio, ayudanos!" A final stroke at the landing gear and the wheels came out. The plane landed safely, and I gave thanks to God. The passengers took their seat belts off quickly, and I was anxious to greet Mr. Graves at the exit door. Captain Graves was six-feet, seven inches tall and had a patch over his right eye. His hand looked like a huge fan. He had a black mustache and a dark black eye. He looked like a pirate. He grabbed my hand and looked me straight in the eye and said, "Have a great summer in New York," and I said, "Thank you."

Freddie, the pastor's nephew, came to pick me up at the airport. He hugged me so hard that I noticed something strange in his demeanor. He was clean-shaven and spoke about entering West Point without finishing his high school diploma. From his incoherent monologue, I knew that Freddie was on something. A few minutes into the Brooklyn-Queens Expressway, and Freddie was offering me cocaine. I refused his offer. I could not believe this was happening again. When we arrived at Pastor Louie's house, his wife, Aida, took me aside and warned me about Freddie. She left me in charge of him, and I quietly thought it was going to be a long summer.

They called him a nephew, but he was really the son of a long-time member from the congregation whom the Pastors were trying to help. His parents had given up all hope, and Pastor Louie came to the rescue. He had helped other young men before, and Freddie was like a son to him, but even for him, Freddie could not be managed.

One hot humid summer day Freddie and I went to buy back light fuses for his 1977 Dodge Charger. The Charger had a 445 motor and burned rubber at the touch of the pedal. Freddie bought the fuses while I waited inside the Charger. He instructed me to take over the steering wheel while he went to the back of the car to check the reverse lights. When I put the car in reverse with the brakes on, the Charger burned rubber and crashed Freddie into the car parked behind his. He screamed and yelled, but everything happened so fast that I only had enough time to put the car in drive. Freddie came down to the ground. An old blue-eyed man with white silver hair appeared out of nowhere and held him before he hit the sidewalk. I tried to figure out what had happened and noticed that I had forgotten to take the brake lock out from the steering wheel. Freddie was twisting and turning with pain. The blood that came out his knees was like a river coming down wild from the mountains. I took my shirt off and held it tightly around one of his legs and screamed for help. The ambulance came, and they took him to Misericordia Hospital in the Bronx. I drove behind the ambulance and went over the scene a dozen times or more.

We made it to Misericordia Hospital in ten minutes. I parked the Charger and ran into the hospital. I called his uncle, Pastor Louie, but he was nowhere to be found. The head nurse in charge of the emergency room, DJ, was an ex-member of the Pastor's church. DJ rushed out of the lab with bad news.

"Junior, preliminary x-rays reveal that Freddie's leg is in critical condition. Doctors need to x-ray him again, but it looks like he may be paralyzed for life. One of the doctors said that if he's lucky, he'll have a broken leg." I was numb. How would I explain this to his uncle? I was left in charge of him.

"DJ are you sure?"

"We need to wait for the second round of x-rays, but all we can do is pray."

DJ had lost all faith in prayer just a few months before. DJ and Sue were a lovely happily married couple of eight years. They both worked at the same hospital, but he worked from 11:00 pm to 7:00 am in the morning, and she worked from 3:00 pm to 11:00 pm. He replaced her every night, and they exchanged kisses in the hallway. They were very active in church, and everyone admired their dedication. Sue was a beautiful green-eyed brunette of five feet, seven inches, and he was handsome, had dark eyes and was close to six feet tall. They made a handsome couple and were the envy of the congregation.

One night while DJ worked his shift, he felt the urge to go home for a quick break. It had been weeks since he had seen his gorgeous wife in bed, and he was dying to see her asleep in their huge bed. The apartment was only five minutes away from Misericordia Hospital, and he drove his 1970 Mustang faster than usual. When he arrived, he noticed the lights of the bedroom on. Sue was an avid reader and spent endless nights reading the classics, and DJ smiled at the thought of her love of Shakespearean sonnets. He quietly went in the apartment and made his way to the master bedroom. As he tiptoed through the apartment, he noticed two half-filled glasses of wine on the kitchen counter. He remembered his wife always drank a glass of Mateus Rose before she went to sleep. Before he turned the doorknob, he heard noises coming from inside his bedroom. He opened the door and was ready to say surprise when he saw his beautiful Sue tangled up in bed with another woman. Words were unnecessary. DJ packed his bags while Sue and her companion watched in terrified silence. DJ continued to work at the hospital, but Sue moved out of town in fear of embarrassment.

I prayed for a miracle. I called Pastor Louie and explained the situation. He listened but was not surprised at the events unfolding. He advised that I was not to let family or friends come close to Freddie. He said he would explain later. An hour later, Freddie was still in the x-ray room. A couple of hours later, Pastor Louie arrived at the hospital. I waited for him outside the hospital and thought of a logical explanation to give him. He did not let me explain, "Junior, I was praying last night, and God told me that Freddie would have an accident, but nothing would happen to him. Call me when he comes out of the x-ray room and come and get the station wagon to take him home. Like I said on the phone, do not let any relatives or friends come to see Freddie. He will be OK".

Another hour went by and my mind was confused but hopeful that God would come through for Freddie. At two minutes before midnight, DJ came out of the x-ray room with a cheek-to-cheek smile on his face. "Junior, I can't believe it, Freddie has only bruises. It's a miracle!" That same night I went to get the station wagon at Pastor Louie's house, and I drove Freddie home. It was a crazy night. Before Freddie went to sleep, we cried and hugged each other. We were all witnesses of this incredible act of Faith. DJ was Freddie's first visitor in the morning. He still could not get over the miracle. He repeated constantly. "I can't believe it!"

A month later, and I was ready to go back to "The Island of Enchantment." Freddie was already walking around with the help of a cane and going out with his girlfriend. Freddie, cane, and all took me to John F. Kennedy Airport. He picked up a girl that was wondering around the neighborhood and asked me to sit in the back of the car while he shared some of our summer incidents with his newly found friend. I spoke very little along the way but noticed Freddie much too interested in his new companion. Freddie and I hugged and said goodbye. It was an unusual summer that neither of us would ever forget.

The DC-10 zoomed through the skies and made it to San Juan thirty minutes ahead of time. My family was there, and I felt relieved to be back home.

GETTING AHEAD

It was in August of 1984 when I met Maria; she was a beauty. She was sixteen years old, and I was twenty-one. I met her at church. She was light-skinned, five feet, three inches tall and hazel eyes, a guitar-like body and natural blonde hair. She was a typical Puerto Rican girl with a touch of the American ideal woman. It was a while before I learned that she was sixteen years old, but it was too late. She was already in my heart and part of my everyday thoughts. I don't know what hit me, but she became my new inspiration.

I had met a few girls at the University, but her simple nature and strong family values won me over. She had three sisters and a younger brother, and her parents were humble and down-to-earth people. Don Jose moved his family from the Northeast to the East because he had received an offer from his millionaire boss, Roger La Fountaine. Mr. La Fountaine bought an estate in Luquillo, Puerto Rico, and he needed Don Jose to be his property manager. The offer included living facilities for his family and a reasonable monthly income. He accepted, and that is how Maria's family moved closer to where I lived during the time.

It was also my senior year at the university, and I needed inspiration and a whole lot more to finish my studies. I started to reflect on a future. Finishing my degree was an immediate goal. The pressure of getting ahead was exhausting. I started thinking of formalizing my relationship with Maria and getting married. I graduated with honors at the University of Puerto Rico, Rio Piedras Campus in 1986. My mother graduated the year before. My girlfriend and mother attended my college graduation. I spent the three hours of the ceremonies thinking about my future. My sweetheart had graduated from high school the month before, and I was planning our wedding for that December. She was young, but I loved her and knew that she was the one I wanted to spend the rest of my life with.

I started working as an English teacher in the public schools of Puerto Rico in January of 1986. One of the cruel realities of teaching in Puerto Rico is salary. Teachers´ salaries were $775.00 a month. I remember my first day well because while driving back home in my mother's 1984 Mazda I had an accident. I hit a policeman from behind. It was my first day on the job, and I was already in debt. My first paycheck came in April and half of it went to the policeman. I wanted to marry my girl, so I took up a part-time teaching job in a private school, and I started saving money for the wedding.

I got married in December of 1986. I always wanted an old-fashioned girl, but it meant that I had to work harder. I carried the financial burden of the wedding, and I was deeply in debt. My landlord was a secretary for the President of Club Rio Mar. It was a hotel resort with a golf course designed by the legendary senior golf legend, Chi Chi Rodriguez and just 45 minutes from San Juan. My landlord's boss, Mr. James Walton, wanted to learn Spanish, and my landlord thought I would make a good Spanish teacher. After a few weeks of Spanish lessons, Mr. Walton offered me a full-time management position as his assistant. He gave me an office, a company car and petty cash to spend at will. It was my dream job. I thought of students moaning and disrupting, and I didn't think twice. I quit teaching and became Dalton's assistant. He also baptized me as the new purchasing agent. A month later, I was given another responsibility, assistant business manager. I had an agenda with at least thirty-six things that I did at the same time, and I was going mad. Instead of having students disrupting, I had grown men who hated my guts because a newcomer was giving them orders. I was working seven days a week, and I was on call twenty-four hours a day. I had no time for my wife, and our honeymoon turned into a nightmare after just a few months at Club Rio Mar.

One year was enough for me at Rio Mar. I quit during the summer of 1988. During that year, the New York City Board of Education had come to Puerto Rico looking for Bilingual teachers. I was impressed with the $23,000.00 -a-year salary with fringe benefits. My marriage was on the rocks, and I believed it could benefit from a new setting. Maria was unhappy because she had not had a child, and I prayed to God and asked Him for a sign. If my wife got pregnant, it meant we had to stay in Puerto Rico. If she did not get pregnant in a period of six months, it meant we had the green light to move to New York. A month later, my wife gave me the good news, but I decided to move to The Big Apple anyway.

Our parents and in-laws were not too happy about us moving to New York. Their first grandson was going to be born in eight months, but I told them we would bring the baby to Puerto Rico for his presentation. I convinced my wife by telling her that I had lots of friends in New York. I lied. I needed an excuse to escape. Throughout the years, my friends and I had gone separate ways. I tried calling them and writing letters to stay in touch, but they never seemed to stay in contact. I loved them all, but we were from different worlds. We packed our bags and headed to New York. Deep in my heart, I knew New York was different, but I was twenty-three years old, and I was inspired by the so-called American Dream. I had mixed emotions while reflecting on the plane ride to Kennedy Airport. Maria was nineteen years old and had never been to New York. Quietly, I knew I was moving in disobedience, but I wanted to defy God.

When we arrived at Kennedy Airport, our friends forgot to pick us up at the airport. Two hours had gone by, and no one showed face. I called my buddies, and they were all sleeping. Finally, Luisito came by in his 1987 Chevy Blazer blasting a hit song by Terence Trent Darby: "sign your name across my heart, I want you to be my baby, sign your name across my heart, I want you to be my baby." He said he was sorry, but I did not hear sincerity in his voice. We stayed with my childhood Pastor Louie for a month and later rented an apartment in the Knickerbockers section of Brooklyn.

It was on the second floor of an old two-story house. Every time I walked up the stairs, the house moved like a swing. The landlords complained about my snoring. The floor trembled with my steps, but it was the best we could afford for $500.00 a month. The landlords were a retired couple from Puerto Rico who had made their living in New York.

After two months of adjusting, moving and getting acquainted with the New York City way of life, it was time to work. The New York City Board of Education hired me to work at Southern Bronx High in the Bronx. The school was right in the middle of the largest Latino communities in the Bronx, and I was looking forward to the experience. When I knocked on the front door the first day of class, I was confused for the new custodian. With that in mind, I was introduced to Mr. Quezada, the Assistant Principal. In many public schools, assistant principals had a more influential role than principals. This was the case at Southern Bronx High. Mr. Quezada was as thin as a needle. He wore a Puerto Rican guayabera, which made me feel at ease, and was very careful with his words.

"Mr. Hernandez, there seems to be a problem here."

"What's the problem?"

"We don't have a position for you here."

"I don't understand. I signed a contract in Puerto Rico."

"We don't have a copy or an original for that matter."

"There must be a mistake."

"Mr. Hernandez, it's simple; we don't have a job in this school for you. Can you teach Math or Science? We may be able to dig up a program for you."

"But I'm not a Science teacher, and I hate Math."

"How about Social Studies? I have always loved history."

"I don't know about that. I'm sorry Mr. Hernandez, take it or leave it. There is really nothing else we can do."

The teacher's lounge was terribly damp. I sat down in a corner sofa, put my head down in between my legs and cried. I don't remember ever crying, but I could not hold back the tears this time. After a short period of prayer and frustration, I remembered I had the telephone number of my recruiter in a piece of paper tucked in my wallet. I called his office and told him of my troubles at Southern Bronx High. He told me to call back in half an hour. The half hour seemed like an eternity. Thanks to my recruiter, I was finally placed at James Monroe High School.

This time the assistant principal, Ms. Laura Gonzalez received me with a nice warm smile. It was very difficult not to notice Ms. Gonzalez. She was forty-something, weighed about one hundred and thirty-five pounds, had light-brown hair and sparkling green eyes. She walked with an air of confidence that kept all her teachers in awe. She was a versatile woman, doubling as an ESL teacher as well as Assistant Principal. My teaching skills were polished at Monroe. Ms. Gonzalez made every effort to make me feel comfortable as a professional. She made unannounced visits that kept you on your toes. I got involved in extra-curricular activities and organized an ESL journalism club. I enjoyed my teaching experience there and felt at home.

One day, the ESL Program at Monroe invited a Puerto Rican poet, Lalo Latorre. I observed him while he got ready. Latorre was dark-skinned with medium height and had black curly hair and deep brown eyes. He dressed completely in white and looked like a Santeria priest. He came in the library with drums and a guitar. I was anxious to hear the poet do his thing. When he started reciting his poetry, he read verses in English and Spanish. He combined music and verses. He closed his eyes as if evoking some supernatural spirit. The students loved what they heard, and I was amazed at their reaction. I identified with the message, and I was curious to know who he was and to know more about his poetry. Mr. Latorre and I became friends, and he gave me a list of Latino writers who were writing and performing in the United States and abroad. Next day, I went to the bookstore and bought a few of the books recommended by Latorre.

My professional career was on a roll, but my marriage and spiritual life were suffering greatly. In three years in the city, we moved five times. Between vacations and deaths in the family, we spent three full months in Puerto Rico in 1990. There was always some reason to go back to Puerto Rico.

In December of 1990, my grandmother Carmelita passed away. The first thing that I remembered about her was the garden. Who would take care of it now? I wondered. I fell asleep during the three-hour flight to the Island. I dreamed of flying over the garden. From the sky, the garden looked like a colorful and glowing rainbow. I felt happy and joyful in the dream. My wife woke me up after the plane had landed at the San Juan airport. Everybody was at the funeral. My aunts and uncles were all dressed in black. There was a lot of crying and yelling. She was loved by everyone. Everybody remembered Carmelita's struggles and how she brought up the children alone. What I remembered the most about her was how she spoke to her flowers every day. There was pain and sorrow when they laid her casket full of flowers in the big black seven-foot hole in the cemetery. Everybody cried. As the first grandson, I shared some last words. Carmelita's garden lived forever.

All my savings were spent on vacations to The Island. The more money I earned, the more I spent. After three years of going nowhere, I decided it was time to move to Puerto Rico. There was no point in living outside of the Island if we were going to go back there three times a year.

COMING HOME

Home at last. I had many friends and relatives in Puerto Rico, and many of them thought I had come back a loser. I experienced that same attitude before, so I prepared myself mentally for this homecoming experience. At first, we stayed with our parents and in-laws. We finally found an apartment in a rural neighborhood of Luquillo called "Mata de Platano". I found a teaching job in a private school in San Juan. It was an hour car drive to and from work, but there was nothing else available. The paycheck was just enough for our weekly sustenance.

In the spring of 1993, I was accepted as a transfer student at the University of Puerto Rico, Rio Piedras Campus, and I was given the opportunity to work as a teaching assistant. My dream of teaching courses at UPR was about to come true. I also contacted my graduate advisor at Herbert H. Lehman College in the Bronx and began planning to go back to New York City to complete my master's thesis the following year. The Director of the Department of English at UPR had offered me a position if I finished my thesis before the school year began. It was the opportunity of a lifetime, a dream come true. I desperately wanted to teach in my alma mater.

When I told the director of the private school, I was going to New York during the summer to finish my degree, she said if I went to study, I would not get paid during the summer, and my teaching contract for August of the following school year could be suspended. I practically begged her to let me go study and come back, but she stressed that if I went to New York City she no longer needed my services as a teacher. I needed the financial support desperately. My thesis could take at least two months of intensive research and writing, and my wife and son depended on my salary for their sustenance. All the moving around had made a heavy dent in my finances, and I lived and survived from paycheck to paycheck. A Master's meant a new future and a step ahead in my career. I sold one of my two cars, made advanced payments on some of my bills and purchased an airline ticket to New York City.

It was a short drive to Luis Muñoz Marin Airport, but my wife's silence made it feel like a thousand years. My five-year-old son seemed confused when I told him I would be going to New York City to finish my studies. Joey was an intelligent young boy and was always curious about my running around. I hugged my wife and kissed my son goodbye. We held back the tears, but my heart sank to my feet. She drove away, and I could only think of the many goodbyes I had made before. It seemed like a rerun from a classic television soap opera.

I took a train from John F. Kennedy Airport to my aunt's apartment in Brooklyn. Aunt Barbarita lived in Flushing Avenue. It was a public building complex. She lived there ever since she lost her previous apartment to a fire sixteen years before. Her neighbors were African Americans and Latinos. The great majority lived on welfare, including my aunt, and public assistance programs. I slept on the sofa bed in the living room. It was wiry and cold, making it very uncomfortable to sleep. As I turned and twisted during the night, I heard firecrackers jittering the neighborhood, and I woke up and called my aunt to ask her about the celebration. She said the firecrackers were the sounds of submachine guns firing away between drug gangs and their neighborhood rivals.

Early next day, I left for Herbert H. Lehman College on Bedford Park Boulevard in the Bronx. Lehman was right on the outskirts of the Bronx. The historic campus was founded in 1931 as the Bronx campus of Hunter College. In 1968, it was established as an independent college of The City University of New York and named after Herbert H. Lehman, the great New York Governor, U.S. Senator, philanthropist, and humanitarian. During World War II, Lehman's campus became the main national training site for women in the military. For a period of six months in 1946, the campus became interim headquarters for the newly formed United Nations. I loved the sight and history of the campus and to come back to complete my thesis in seven weeks was a challenge, but I had the intention of meeting the expectations of the situation and come back to my family with a graduate degree.

I planned to meet with my graduate advisor. Mrs. Dixon was in her late sixties, and she walked with the help of a cane, but she was a very business-like and energetic woman. We arranged to meet at 9:00 am in her office, and she was already revising papers as I walked in sharply. I greeted her, and she looked at me very sternly and said,

"How much time are you planning to stay in New York?"

"I plan to revise proofread and hand-in the final paper in seven weeks."

"What? Are you insane?"

"I must go back to Puerto Rico by August 13."

"That's impossible! It will take at least another six months to write a paper like that."

"It's an act of Faith."

"I don't understand. There is no way you can do this!"

"I will finish the thesis in seven weeks."

"Mr. Hernandez, you need more than Faith to write a paper."

Obstacle number one: there was no professor to revise and proofread my thesis. Mrs. Dixon said that the only professor available was the Chair of the Department of English. After an hour explaining my situation, I finally convinced her to help me. Obstacle number two: I was running out of funds. Registration was about $700.00, and I had $500.00 cash in my pocket. When I went to pay for registration and other graduate fees, a clerk at the Bursar put her job on the line by writing down that a special grant would pay for half of registration. That gave me four weeks to get the other half of the registration. A few weeks later, my sister Elbita sent me the other half of the money. Obstacle number three: I was computer illiterate. I walked down the hallway and identified a Math professor. He had to know something about computers. I respectfully approached him and explained the situation, and much to my surprise, he gladly spent an hour of his time and gave me a crash course on computers. It was a do or die, and I learned how to work with the computer.

The seven weeks in New York were simply unbelievable. I applied for food stamps and was approved $80.00. I gave my Aunt half of the money and with the other half I bought a ham and cheese sandwich every day for lunch. The sandwich cost two dollars, and somehow the $40.00 got me through the complete seven weeks of lunches. I gobbled down the sandwiches with water for lunch. I was able to apply for unemployment benefits. When the money came in, I sent it to Puerto Rico. All in all, I survived and so did Maria and Joey in Puerto Rico.

A few days before I completed my master's thesis, I called my ex-babysitter, Dorcas, and she invited me over her house for a weekend. I needed to get away for at least a weekend. Angel and Dorcas lived in Suffern, New York. Suffern is a small town about thirty-minutes east of New York City. They lived in the Bronx since they were married in 1975. They were teachers in the New York City school system and spent years saving money to buy a house and safely bring up their two children outside of the city. The decision to move out of the city was not well received by either of the Valentin children. Andy was only eight years old but protested vehemently, and fifteen-year-old Sara threatened to move in with her New York City friends, but she eventually supported the family decision. For them, Suffern meant a new beginning.

It was a cool early summer day. The bus cruised swiftly over the George Washington Bridge and went from town to town until the bus driver called Suffern. I was the only passenger getting off the old and lop-sided bus. I put my backpack on my shoulder and walked into town. After six-weeks in New York City, I had grown an Afro and a goatee. I had on an old pair of jeans and a long blue shirt. I reached for the paper in my pocket with Dorcas' address. The town looked like a Tarrytown replica, and I quickly felt at home. As I looked for the paper where I had Dorcas' address, a policeman drove by, made a u-turn and parked his car next to me.

"Excuse me, you looking for somebody?"

"Actually yes, I just got in from the city."

"Listen here, fellar, this here is a small country town."

"Sir, I'm here on a weekend visit."

"I don't really care, mister. You better not cause any trouble. We don't like strangers roaming about town."

"No sir, I won't."

"Where you going?"

"My ex-baby-sitter's house, Dorcas."

"Yeah, I figured, that's those "Porto Ricans", they the only ones in town. Why don't you hop on, I'll take yaw'?" I was tentative but decided to follow his suggestion. He said his name was John Robinson. His father moved from Southern Mississippi thirty years before. He apologized for being hard on me but explained that it was his duty to keep the town safe and sound of strangers and common criminals. I kept quiet and listened while he turned into my friends' house. He parked right in front of Dorcas' house, and I apprehensively shook his hands. I carefully got out of the car, walked up the driveway to the front door and rang the bell. Officer Robinson slowly shifted the steering wheel but looked on while I rang the bell again. Before I rang it again, she opened the door. Robinson finally took off when she greeted me with a hug. I let out a huge sigh of relief.

She explained that Robinson was the only police officer in town, and he often picked up strangers and led them out of town. She said she forgot to warn me but promised making it up to me by being a great host. I finally sat down, got comfortable and enjoyed the evening with my hosts. I had a wonderful time, just talking, eating in and going out for a slice of pizza or two. On Sunday afternoon, Angel and Dorcas drove me to the train station and left when I stepped into the Metro-North express train.

My thesis was approved on August 11, 1994. Mrs. Dixon could not believe it. I heard her saying that it was a miracle. I was happy but mentally exhausted by all the reading, writing and intensive research that I had gone through. But I had declared the victory by Faith. I called my wife and family in Puerto Rico and gave them the good news. I took the shuttle train from Brooklyn to John F.

Kennedy Airport. The plane ride was swift and smooth, and my heart shifted gears when I saw the Dorado, Puerto Rico beach sea line from 5,000 feet. The plane landed, and everyone applauded, and I joined in clapping my hands like never. I ran out the gate and quickly spotted my beautiful Maria and my son Joey in her arms. I was almost stuck in between a revolving door at the airport, but I pushed it open with a forward thrust. All this coming back and forth, and I had come back victorious.

GROUND ZERO

After five years of striving for a tenure-track position at the University of Puerto Rico, I rethought my priorities. At thirty-six years of age, I was full of energy and healthy. As Director of the largest college student exchange program in Puerto Rico, I achieved what my ambitions desired: control, power and status, but the dream job had become hectic and extremely stressful. I was the director of the largest student exchange programs in the Caribbean, and my responsibilities were making a dent in my personal relationships, especially in my marriage. I worked overtime every day, and I was always late for dinner or for my son's after school activities. Maria wanted more time, and I was in the middle of a tug of war at home.

One evening, Pablo, an ex-change student attending a university in a Western state called me at seven at night. I was still in the office:

"Professor, how are you doing? asked Pablo desperately."

"Hi, Pablo, you sound worried."

"Professor, I just got back from the police station."

"Calm down, Pablo. What happened?"

"I was walking down the street just a block away from the dorms when a policeman stopped me."

"What did you do? Did you violate any law? You know how much we've warned you here at the office."

"No, I didn't violate any law. The cop asked me for the green card" replied Pablo nervously.

"What?"

"That's the same way I reacted."

"I told him that I was Puerto Rican, and Puerto Rico had a Commonwealth Government, and we were American citizens."

"And…?"

"He did not understand. He said as far as he was concerned, I needed proof of American citizenship, and he asked me for an identification card. I had left my identification cards in the dorms. I started explaining in my Puerto Rican English, but he did not understand. Finally, I got a little angry, lost control of myself. He called for backup and arrested me."

"Oh, my God!"

"That's right. I was handcuffed, read my rights, and taken to the police station. I was allowed a phone call, so I called my roommate who ran into the police headquarters with my life-saving driver's license. He spoke English fluently and was able to explain our situation as Puerto Ricans to the local town precinct."

While listening to Pablo, I remembered how nervous his mother had been about the student exchange experience. She migrated from Mexico to California in the late 1970's. In California, she married a wealthy Puerto Rican businessman and later came to Puerto Rico with her husband. While living in California, her husband was on a business trip to New York and in an immigration raid in the restaurant where she worked as a part-time waitress, she was arrested and sent back to Mexico. After a two-month ordeal, she was finally cleared and allowed to return to California with her husband and family, but the experience marked her forever.

After hanging up the phone with Pablo, I felt a strange pain in my chest. I knew it was only a cramp, but with this kind of stress, this job was going to take away more than just my health and family. I had two secretaries, an administrative assistant and two program directors. The complaints and animosity between them were driving me crazy. They hated each other's guts, and it was driving me up the wall.

There were approximately one hundred fifty exchange students on Campus from universities all over the world, adult teenage students who came to Puerto Rico looking for a year of excitement and adventure. There were also about one hundred and fifty UPR students spread around the world and close to two hundred foreign students whom we attended and facilitated their stay. On one hand, there were young Puerto Rican college students who spent a year away from their cradles. On the other, there were American and foreign students looking for a taste of paradise. Sometimes the excitement turned into trouble, and I had to be on alert twenty-four hours a day. On top of that, I had a position in trust of the Chancellor, which meant I had no job security. My employees knew that I was not in-house permanently, and they questioned my authority and decisions constantly. I worked twelve to fourteen hours a day and traveled abroad at least once every two months. I was heading into a collision course drive without any brakes to save me from disaster.

In July of 1999, the new Campus Chancellor asked the Deans for their resignations. The Assistant Dean of students met with me and asked about my plans. I got the message. A few days later, I donated blood for my father's open-heart surgery, and the nurse informed me that my blood pressure was rocket high. She took my blood because it was an emergency but recommended, I see a doctor as soon as possible.

Three days later, I received an invitation for a teaching position in a junior high school just minutes from my home. I considered my options and believed that my life could benefit from a new beginning. I really had accepted this appointment as a challenge, but I was not an administrator. My employees were driving me mad; I was and will always be a teacher at heart. In August of 1999, I met with my staff and broke the news:

"Due to personal reasons, today is my last day as the Director of the student exchange program. Tomorrow I return to my roots, teaching English in the public schools."

"Professor, after all you've done," said Deborah with tears in her eyes.

"I know this catches you by surprise, but I want to begin again. Life is a cycle."

"Come on, Professor, isn't there really another reason why you are resigning?" inquired Linda suspiciously.

"The reason is that I want to go back to the beginning and refocus my priorities. My wife and son need me now more than ever. I need to put my life in order before I lose it all. That's the real reason I am resigning."

"Can we do anything to make you stay?" asked María with worried eyes.

"I appreciate your support, hard work and dedication, but my decision is final. Linda, please put all my papers in order."

It was more difficult for me than it was for them. I was letting go of my ideal and comfortable position. Although I was not teaching full-time, I did get the opportunity to teach a course that I had created during my previous tour of duty in 1996. In other words, I was once more letting go of my dream come true opportunity. For me, it was a comfort zone that soon turned my life into a war zone. But the job had turned me away from my values, spiritual roots, and my family. I spent the rest of the afternoon cleaning my office and reflecting on the days ahead.

It was raining cats and dogs the day I drove into Alma Dolores Fernandez Santiago Junior High School. The school was one of the largest and oldest schools in the Fajardo region. Students that attended were mostly from impoverished neighborhoods and broken homes. There were so many students. They looked like ants in a swarm. I was dazed and dizzy when I got out of the car on the first day of class. I observed the muddy parking lot, and I glanced at the old and tainted walls, the ghetto classrooms, and the abandoned basketball court. It was a long way from Tarrytown. The school looked like an old medieval castle. I opened the trunk of my car, picked up my suitcase and walked towards the Principal's Office. I noticed graffiti on the wall while my new shoes were already full of mud. I hurried my pace and walked into the Principal's Office. As I walked into the office, all eyes turned on me, and there was dead silence. The secretary rushed me into the Principal's Office.

The Principal, Mrs. Awilda Flores Sanchez, was a legend in the public schools in Fajardo. She was well into her late seventies but had the energy and health of a forty-year-old woman. She was barely five feet tall, walked with a cane and wore tailor made clothes. She had red hair that matched her nail polish, jewelry, and accessories with the color of her clothes. She sat behind a tower shaped desk and said good morning with a stern and rigid face.

"Well, well, well, Mr. Hernández, an ex-professor and ex-director at the University of Puerto Rico" she said with a smile that reminded me of my graduate advisor, Mrs. Dixon.

"That's right, but I am willing to learn and adapt."

"I'll tell you something. I don't care if you were a professor at the university, director of a student exchange program and writer. In this school, you are a rookie" she said putting her fist on top of the desk.

"Mrs. Flores, the experience that I have gained through the years will help me to cope."

"That's nice but remember two things: I am the boss, and I give the orders around here. You do as you are told. I don't know if I have a room for you. Worse comes to worse, you'll be roaming from one classroom to the next. That's the best that I can do for you. Take it or leave it."

"I'll take it."

Mrs. Flores started rambling about the school, its history and the students, but I wasn't listening. I decided to forget about Mrs. Flores and focus on the students. New beginnings aren't always easy, and I knew by the sound of my new boss that this was going to be a process.

My classroom experience was enlightening. The students were restless but interested in the activities I shared with them. When I was introduced to the faculty, no one said hello or greeted me. There was a look of bewilderment in most of my colleague's faces. Most of them had attended my workshops in the past. After the meeting was over, a member of the English staff approached me and asked:

"What the hell are you doing here?" she nervously lit a cigarette.

"It's a spiritual experience" I replied immediately.

"What! You got to be crazy to come here" said the teacher.

"I'm looking forward to the experience."

"Go away. Get out of my way. You're crazy!" she said and ran down the slippery hallway.

I was mentally prepared for the homecoming. They did not understand what an ex-university professor and lecturer was doing in middle school with a bad reputation. They thought I had fallen from grace and kept their distance from me. I did not let that distract me. For me, it was ground zero and now it was time to build a foundation.

I began using short stories, essays and poetry written by United States Puerto Rican and Latino/writers. My years of teaching in New York City had introduced me to a new literature: the literature of the Puerto Rican and Latino/a experience in the United States. The literature was virtually unknown in Puerto Rico. The student enjoyed stories with young adult characters as protagonists, poetry with music and sound, plays with real-life dramas in them, and I was satisfied. When I observed the glitter in their eyes after I read and sang "Boricua", a free-spirit, free-verse poem by Tato Laviera, I knew that I had made the right decision to start all over again.

After a semester of getting acquainted with the school, the students and Mrs. Flores, I sent a proposal to the Office of Professional Staff Development of the City of New York. The good news came in early April of 2000; I was hired by the Office of High Schools/Bilingual Programs of the City of New York to present a one-week Institute titled, *Integrating United States Puerto Rican Literature in the ESL Classroom.* I was going back to New York, one more time.

My wife drove me to Isla Verde Airport in Carolina. María was accustomed to my New York escapades, and she wasn't worried. I observed my gorgeous María while she maneuvered the steering wheel. She had just turned thirty and was more beautiful than ever. Her hazel eyes sparkled with the reflection of the sun. Her lips were soft and round. We hugged each other and said goodbye again. I swallowed hard and tried not to cry, but Maria let a lonely tear come down her rosy cheek. She drove off, and I went to check-in. In Carolina, the late morning afternoon rain thundered down. I put my mind on the work ahead.

Whenever I traveled alone, I always wondered who my next-seat neighbor on the plane will be. I felt lucky when a young and attractive woman sat next to me. She said hello, and I returned the greeting. She looked like an Italian goddess with radiant light green eyes and sparkling blonde hair. She said that she was in Puerto Rico on business and was very angry about her brief experience on the Island. I picked on her lead and continued the conversation with her.

"This sure isn't New York" she said, looking relieved.

"No, it ain't" I replied.

"I was here on business for a few days, and I nearly got raped and assaulted" she said with anger.

"I'm sorry to hear that" I replied.

"I hate Puerto Rico" she uttered with bitterness.

"Puerto Ricans are a wonderful race and Puerto Rico is a beautiful place. What happened?"

"Well, I went for an early morning walk on the beach, and these two natives started yelling things at me."

"What do you mean? How were you dressed?"

"I wore one of my conservative bikinis."

"That explains it. With all due respect, you are a very beautiful woman. Puerto Rican men cannot stay quiet when observing a doll like you in a bathing suit. It's in our blood to say something."

"Well, I don't care, they were disrespectful. I felt naked and overwhelmed. I believe they mentioned something about my hips, and I ran back to the hotel. What an awful experience!"

"I can tell you more about the Puerto Rican culture."

"It's a long story, and I don't know if you have the time."

"Hey, I've got three hours."

"You sure you wanna hear this."

"Go ahead."

Alma reclined her seat, and I proceeded to tell her the story. But it was not just a story, but a story about the beginnings of the so-called Rican. He was a fictional character based on pieces of information I put together through research, documentaries and stories told by aunts and uncles. I planned to work on the draft on the way to and from New York City. Why not take advantage of the moment and read it to someone to get feedback from it now? The story was staged at the end of the nineteenth century. I called it ***The Birth of a Rican.***

Manolo came to the United States of America in the blizzard winter of 1900. Puerto Ricans began migrating to the United States as far back in time as the American Revolutionary War, but it was not until Americans won the Spanish American War, and the Island of Puerto Rico became a U.S. territory that their presence as a community on the United States mainland emerged. The new American military government installed in Puerto Rico in 1898 facilitated a slow yet steady migration.

Manolo's father lost ownership of his property in 1880 to a Spanish landlord in the hills of an eastern coastal town in Puerto

Rico called Naguabo, and he welcomed his newly found American friends with open arms. Don Manuel was anxious to get his farm back and became an ally of the recently appointed authorities. Because of the family's financial decline, young Manolo was asked to drop out of school to help support the family.

Don Manuel never got his land back from the Americans. The new government was accompanied by a group of Americans called capitalists, and one of them bought the 120-acre property at a discount price from the outgoing Spanish landlord. Shortly after, he went bankrupt. Manolo's parents separated, and a great uncle needed help in his farm in the steep Rio Blanco Hills in Naguabo, so he was sent there and worked like a slave. Even with the abolition of slavery, the boy's uncle practically owned the lives of more than fifty mulattos, which Uncle Saul hit with a horse's whip every time they took a break or sat down during the grueling six-day fourteen-hour working week. He was just another mouth to feed and was not discriminated against when Uncle Saul one day caught him taking a quick break and snapped the thick and greasy whip at him with all his strength. The boy's back was split open. His aunt ran with him to the local hospital and got him patched up and ready for work the next day. That was the last time he ever sat down while he worked at his Uncle's ranch.

She was a good listener, but I noticed her sleepy after the first fifteen minutes. When I was halfway through the story, she fell asleep. I couldn't help noticing her clear and smooth skin. Her thick eyebrows were enticing, and her long silky beautiful hair was seducing. I continued to read the story anyway and made believe that she was listening. I knew that one day I would have an audience.

With the change of government, a new immigration package was announced through local town representatives. There was an Island, much like Puerto Rico, they said, and a territory in the Pacific called Hawaii, and Puerto Ricans were being told that they could make a fortune and provide for the well-being of their families there. The Hawaii Sugar Corporation was looking for cheap labor throughout the recently acquired U.S. territories, and friendly recruiters promised comfortable traveling accommodations for the trip and good jobs and a bright future once the migrants arrived and settled.

Manolo was in town running errands for Uncle Saul, and he walked over to the town plaza when he heard the news. He had turned eighteen and was tired of being humiliated, enslaved, and abused by Uncle Saul. This was perfect for an escape. He listened carefully as they explained about the lottery. It was a system where men were chosen to go to Hawaii for their job skills. There was a quota and a week later, Manolo's ticket was not chosen, but his cousin won the ticket one day when he got drunk, Manolo challenged him over a deck of cards and won it back.

In the late Island tropical winter of 1900, 200 men left Puerto Rico en route to Hawaii. In the two-week journey by ship to New Orleans, by train across land to San Francisco, and by ship again to Hawaii, the passengers suffered severe shortages of water and food; only 188 made it alive to the San Francisco coastline. The survivors looked like living skeletons.

It was a thunderous and rainy night when the loud and noisy steamship hit the dock. The Puerto Rican migrants were all lined up like sardines in a can when three hundred American troops greeted them on the boat's platform. The soldiers had stifling bayonets, and Manolo was scared to death. As he walked down the ship's broken wooden stairs and down into the port, the freezing wind felt like it could cut his skin. He had an old worn sweater, and he felt the chilly breeze crawling in every bone of his body. His lips began peeling, his ears were like solid rock, and his knees trembled like an earthquake. Although he was not superstitious, his aunt had taught him to stare at the palm of his hands for good luck and direction. When he looked at the line of the sun in his hands, they seemed to be out of their usual position.

From there, the migrant corpses walked for about two miles under the conspicuous eye of the soldiers. They were taken to giant freight trains. First the troops, then the rifles and now the trains. Manolo was worried. At two o'clock in the morning and while the soldiers slept, he and sixty-nine others jumped off the train and with the help of a compass ran north until early in the morning they reached a small California town. They never made it to Hawaii.

After five months of intense and often heated discussions, debates, and public hearings about whether the so-called "Porto Ricans", as the press called them, should stay or sent back to Puerto Rico, the town council allowed the migrants to stay as long as they agreed to stay away from the town and work in the towering cornfields owned by the Mayor himself. They did not want any trouble and made them swear to keep away from the city limits or else.

The new migrants founded a Puerto Rico of their own in three former barn houses where they rested and slept after the long twelve-hour working days. The salary was five cents more than what Manolo made in Puerto Rico, and he worked for five days only, but he made the best of his situation because he did not want to go back to Puerto Rico. Going back to work for Uncle Saul was simply out of the question.

He noticed her at church. Between the singing and worshipping, Manolo gazed at a young and attractive girl. Maria was a beautiful Christian girl. The pastor had strict seating arrangements. Men and women sat in different aisles of the temple. She was very well guarded and protected, and Maria's parents sat her in between them, making it practically impossible for him to get a look at her. But he stared at her when she got up to sing and pray and could not avoid noticing her rocking hips beneath her pink dress. He thought they were simply enchanting.

She was fifteen years old, and he was twenty, but he could care less. She had olive-skin, five-foot three inches tall with river black eyes, a guitar-like body and long brown semi-curly hair. Maria was a Mexican girl, and her father was the mayordomo of the Mayor's ranch. She was the oldest of seven sisters and the prettiest according to Manolo. There was no way he could get close to her, so he decided to befriend the girl's father. Juan Feliciano was a stern and stubborn man, but Manolo was persistent and little by little earned the respect of the girl's father. He ran errands for him and was the first man on the job in the morning. In the meantime, he had been able to get eye contact and a smile from her in church, and he knew that she too liked him.

The Puerto Ricans got all they needed at the ranch. Don Feliciano, as they called him, was a tough but fair administrator. If they did their work, all was well. The Mayor provided them with food, drinks, and monthly social events. A doctor came around twice a year for routine physical check-ups. It was at one of those parties that Manolo finally got the chance to speak to Maria. They spoke for about an hour, and there was no doubt in his mind that this was the girl he wanted to marry. Maria was an innocent young girl, and Manolo convinced her that he could give her more liberty and freedom than her father. He lied, but he wanted to kiss her, hold her and get a hand on her smooth-looking breasts and plump hips.

Manolo worked side-by-side with Don Feliciano and did everything he could to please the old man. He hated him to death, but it was the only way he could have Maria. It was just a matter of time before he could ask him for the girl's hand. One day while they sat down together in the shade after a long day's work, Manolo took advantage of the old man's good mood and broke the news:

"Don Feliciano, I'd like permission to have your daughter's hand."

"What! Well, I don't know. She's only fifteen."

"Tu eres un viejo".

"I'm twenty."

"Manolo, you're a good man, hard-working and responsible, but I think we should talk about this later."

"No problem."

The old man was not convinced, but Manolo was enthusiastic about the whole thing. He needed a woman, a wife, and a family. After months of mild and sometimes hot discussions, Don Feliciano allowed Manolo to talk to Maria after church services. This was not the best of arrangements, but he knew that in due time, Maria could be his for keeps. After another six months of courtship, Don Feliciano granted her hand. Manolo and María were married on December 27, 1903.

It was a typical Puerto Rican-Mexican American wedding. There were about three hundred guests. Invitations were sent to relatives in Puerto Rico. Only a couple made the long ship ride to attend the wedding. It was a surprise, and Manolo fantasized at the thought of seeing his parents again. But much to his dismay, Uncle Saul and his aunt walked down the port dock. He swallowed hard and hugged him and his loving aunt. Manolo made an extreme effort to bury the pain that he carried in his heart. He still had the one-foot scar across his back. This was a time of joy, and he did not want to spoil the occasion. His parents sent him a deed to a small farm in the forsaken hills in Naguabo, Puerto Rico. He politely received the papers, which granted him ownership of a one-acre lot in a rocky and uphill territory in the so-called Rio Blanco Hills, but he knew that he would never again go back to Puerto Rico.

Maria was an hour and a half late to the wedding, but she made it, and Manolo's stomach twisted and turned when the wedding music announced the bride. The church was packed. All the Puerto Ricans celebrated. He had married the mayordomo's daughter, and his compatriots saw it as a sense of relief. Manolo would be in charge, they thought, after Don Feliciano's death. The old man had been complaining of chest pains lately, and the Puerto Ricans were getting tired of his bullish ways. It was a gathering of sorts, and Manolo had to break up a couple of shuffles between his buddies and the Mexicans. They finally were able to head out to their honeymoon. The Mayor was kind enough to allow them to spend a few days at his summer cottage near the sea. Manolo finally got his woman.

He always wanted an old-fashioned girl, but it meant that he had to work harder. His father-in-law did not improve working conditions, and his fellow Puerto Ricans started to call him a traitor. Don Feliciano got healthier and stronger, and he did not seem close to death at all. Thirty days after the wedding, and María gave Manolo the good news; she was pregnant and quit her job at the ranch. Her belly started jumping during the night, and he barely slept three hours each night. Her mood changes and cravings were getting to him, and he was getting tired of not being able to sleep with her every night. It was getting hectic, and Manolo was already thinking of going back to Puerto Rico, but the idea of becoming a father and his physical need for Maria got him through difficult times, turmoil and hardship.

The boy's birth did not come without pain. Maria's pregnancy went beyond the expected nine months. Exactly twenty-one days after Maria's nine-month of pregnancy, Manolo heard his wife shouting:

"Oh Manolo, it's the baby" cried María with thick tears in her eyes.

"What?" He shouted.

"*Mi amor*, I think it's him. *Ai Dios mio*! I can't take the pain."

"María hold on. Let me get the horses."

"Manolo. I can't wait. Busca a mama."

After a grueling seventy-two hours of child labor, he was born. Everyone on the ranch celebrated his birth. For the Puerto Ricans, it meant hope. For the Mexicans, it was the joy of Don Feliciano's first grandson. Despite the physical difficulties his mother had during her pregnancy, Jose Manuel was a rather healthy and beautiful boy. He weighed eight pounds, twelve ounces and was twenty-two inches long. Manolo combined the names of two of his best friends who died on the trip from Puerto Rico three years before. He wanted an American nickname for his son, so he called him Joey. He was Maria's first and only child. Her pregnancy was so humanly unbearable that they decided not to have a second child. Don Feliciano was outraged at their decision, but Manolo reminded him that he had six other daughters who could give him more grandchildren.

She was a dutiful wife and hardworking mother. Every day she ironed clothes, washed the dishes, and breast-fed Joey, without saying a thing. But time passed, and she started getting tired of cleaning house, doing the laundry, preparing the coffee, caring for the baby, and cooking rice and beans for her husband. Manolo was the moody type and often complained of not getting enough attention from his adorable Mexican girl. He was never satisfied with Maria's devotion and love. There were also arguments between Manolo and his father-in-law. Manolo argued that the old man was always in the middle of everything, and Don Feliciano thought his son-in-law had turned into a *sinverguenza*. There were rumors about his early-hour escapades to the town pubs. Even Maria's sisters felt uncomfortable with Manolo's long and tight hugs. His sister-in-law's had grown into lavishing young women, and he took advantage of every opportunity he got to get physically close to them. Their marriage had turned into a nightmare soon after Joey's birth.

Joey graduated from high school when Puerto Ricans on the Island of Puerto Rico became United States citizens in 1917. It was a big thing for Manolo. The Puerto Ricans had multiplied, and the Mayor found no choice but to allow them to live near the town suburbs. Many of the original seventy had married Mexican girls from the town. Five of Don Feliciano's daughters had married Manolo's compatriots. There were differences within the two communities, but they were able to maintain a cordial friendship that went beyond the disputes over land boundaries, personal relationships, and improved working conditions, which never came.

Manolo had celebrated his fortieth birthday, and it was the right excuse for a new beginning. He had settled down, and his beautiful María had forgiven him for all his mishaps. There was talk about a Puerto Rican migration to New York City. According to the California newspapers, commercial ties and the trading of raw materials opened a new window of opportunity for the new Puerto Rican settlers in New York City. After the United States obtained control of the Island, more working-class Puerto Ricans came to New York.

Manolo saw the events as an opportunity to escape the vigilant and watchful eye of his father-in-law. María struggled to survive in a marriage filled with false promises and a *machista* husband. She sought answers from within but found none. Despite their parents' troubled relationship, Joey did well in school. He had very poor communication with his father but was everything for his mother. She protected her handsome son and made sure he did not turn out like his father. While Manolo used any excuse to start a fight with whomever, the boy stayed away from problems. His friends admired his poise and tranquility. He was often called "The Peacemaker" because he mediated in difficult situations in the neighborhood, especially the clashes between the Puerto Ricans and the Mexicans at the ranch. He was a rare combination. Born American in California of Puerto Rican and Mexican immigrants. But he grew up extremely proud of his American roots. He spoke English at school, but Spanish was the primary language in his house in the neighborhood and at church. He lived in a household where three cultures and two languages became one. There was no fuss or discussion about when to use English or Spanish. It was natural for Joey to speak English with his friends and Spanish with family.

It was right after Joey's high school graduation in 1920 that Manolo broke the good news. He was moving his family to New York City; end of story, no discussions. It was like a bombshell to Maria's family. Don Feliciano put up a fight, but it was Manolo's word that mattered, as always; however, Joey was excited because he had read about the Puerto Rican migration up East and was interested in meeting new people. Moreover, his father convinced him about the better career opportunities he would find in New York City. Since he was in grade school, he had grown up wanting to make a difference, and this was not the place for him to fulfill his dream.

They arrived in New York City in the leafless autumn of 1923. The trees had gown barren faster than usual, leaving a winter touch to an early autumn. Thanks to a cousin who had moved from Puerto Rico a few years before, he rented a small apartment on 110th street off Third Avenue in Manhattan. It was in a block of two-story tenements with brick fronts. The apartment was a two-room second floor walk-up. It had a bedroom, a kitchen-living room, and a bathroom. Joey complained about sleeping in the living room, but his father guaranteed that they would move into a better place soon.

Maria was silent but felt she was living in a fish tank. She was prohibited from leaving the apartment and talking to her neighbors. It was too dangerous, according to her husband, and she spent endless hours looking out the window and cleaning the apartment hundreds of times. Every time she argued with Manolo about New York, he reminded her of the better opportunities that existed for

Joey. She kept quiet and held on to the love that she had for the family.

Manolo bought books for Joey, not many, but enough to spark his son's interest. As his interest grew, his father continued to buy more books for him. The boy enjoyed reading late into the night and encountered an imaginary world that took him away from his parents' everyday differences. The atmosphere at home was not always warm and the American and British classics provided him with comfort and sudden relief. Amongst his favorites were John Milton, Edgar Allan Poe, and William Shakespeare. He was especially fond of a late nineteenth century writer that went by the name of Edwin Arlington Robinson.

Joey found a job at a small cigar shop and was introduced to a group of recently arrived Puerto Rican laborers from the Island who worked rolling tobaccos and read books and talked politics. They taught him the trade, and he learned fast. His co-workers had practically turned the working area into a university. One of them served as a reader, who read to them for one-half hour in the morning and one-half hour in the afternoon. This was unusual for Joey yet exciting because of his fondness for books and knowledge. He was hungry to learn and the whole dynamics of the readings and discussions really sparked his interest and caught his attention.

Much of what they talked about was surreal to him, but he found their conversations amusing. They often tried to drag him into reader-response sessions about whether Puerto Rico should become a United States state, an independent republic or stay as a territory of the United States of America, but Joey could care less. He was an American, he told them, and they politely laughed at his reaction. They claimed he was a new breed. They called him The

Rican. It was a combination of the United States of America, Puerto Rico, and Mexico, they said. He decided to accept the nickname, with which his half-brothers had baptized him with. They were right, he thought. After all, there was something about them that attracted him to them. He was lured by the smell of tobacco and the debates about political issues.

Manolo found a job in an Italian restaurant earning a dollar and fifteen cents a day. He washed dishes, mopped the floors, cleaned the bathrooms, and did everything he was ordered to do. He sometimes worked twelve hours a day but got paid for eight. For his overtime hours, Manolo's boss provided him with leftover meals, which María and Joey devoured during the cold, freezing and hungry winters of the 1920's.

It was during the hot and humid summer of 1925 that Joey fell in love. She was Italian, and the daughter of Manolo's boss, the owner of five of New York City's finest restaurants, which were strategically positioned throughout the city. One day, Joey came by to leave a message from his mother when he saw her for the first time.

She looked like an Italian Goddess from Roman mythology. She had light green radiant eyes and long sensuous black hair. Her legs were perfect, and her waist seemed like a road with smooth curves. Her eyes were deeply expressive but had a profound sadness to them. She was attracted to him immediately. Joey was twenty-two and had never had a girlfriend before. He was about six feet tall, and his tan looking skin had flourished during the summer. His eyebrows were lined up perfectly, and he had a smile that lit up the room wherever he happened to be at the time. She had graduated from high school two years before and helped her father take care of the family business. Rose seemed out of reach for Joey, but he won her over with his warm heart and extraordinary smile.

Rose's father was strongly against the relationship, and he threatened to fire Manolo. He liked him but never imagined his daughter married to a son of a Puerto Rican. He advised Manolo to tell his son to stay away, or else. He was outraged and immediately confronted Joey. He needed the job, he argued, and Joey promised his father that he would stay away. But they continued to meet secretly. They were madly in love and decided to see each other against their parent's will.

Little did Rose know that her father had promised her hand in matrimony to the son of the wealthiest Italian in New York City. Everything had been arranged. Mario Capone, Rose's father, had lost most of the family money in a bad financial deal with a bootlegger in Long Island. This partnership arrangement through marriage deal would stabilize the family financial outlook and put an end to his worries. Someone had to pay the price in the family. It seemed that Rose was falling into an abyss, and Joey dived right into it.

They planned to elope because Mr. Capone would never approve the relationship, and they loved each other too much to break up. They met secretly in parks. They had few options, but they wanted to marry, live together, and have a family.

Mario Capone, the Italian entrepreneur, was well known in Manhattan. He was an icon to the Italians in Hell's Kitchen. Although he was extremely powerful, he had risen from a very humble background. His father and brothers had all worked for New York Central railroad. But young Mario wanted better, and as a child, worked in a restaurant and became the owner's apprentice. The owner had no children and treated Mario as one of his own.

Right at the turn of the twentieth century, the owner and his wife were assassinated by Italian mobsters, and twenty-year old Mario found himself at the helm of the restaurant. He hired his brothers and transformed the place into one of New York's best restaurants. He bought another restaurant near Yankee Stadium and made good contacts within the Bronx Bomber organization. Many of the pinstripe regulars dined at Capone's. From there, he continued networking and opened three more restaurants. But too many city regulations and a lifestyle of fame and fortune, made him make financial arrangements with loan sharks and bootleggers, and his once stable empire had fallen in economic disarray.

After their relationship blossomed, Mr. Capone broke the news to Rose. He had promised her to the son of the wealthy Louie Righetti. Louie Jr. was the sole heir of the Righetti fortune. Rose was in shock but kept quiet. Her relationship with Joey did not exist in her father's mind. She was never allowed to have a say or a word in her father's decisions, especially since Capone had vehemently disapproved of her previous relationship and had banished her on a two-year exile in Italy. She loved Joey but had to obey her father.

Joey was flabbergasted when Rose shared the news. He tried to convince her to go to California with him. They could begin a new life there, he argued. But she did not want to leave her life in New York City. She loved him, but there had to be other alternatives. He had become an excellent cigar roller and had been trained and ready to start a new business. It was the opportunity that his father had mentioned, and this was the right time. The trade of his half-brothers from the Island had found a space in his heart. When his half-brothers observed his determination to learn the trade, they reminded him of his Puerto Rican roots. It was in his blood, they said. Joey laughed but became more and more thoughtful about their claims. There was something about them that made him identify with their talk, walk and way of life.

Joey's Puerto Rico was all comprised in telegrams about deaths in the family, newspaper stories about the U.S. invasion of the new New York migrants and stories he heard from Manolo about a great-uncle and a farm in a nightmarish mountain that his father never forgot. It was a fantasy island to him. The more his co-workers spoke about the place, the more he developed for experiencing it. Now that Rose was deep in his heart, his spirit dwindled when he considered moving to the Caribbean Island. But it was an option for a new beginning.

California was his birthplace and the land of his upbringing, and he had left friends and family behind, but he felt like there was a piece of him still missing. Maria knew about her son's relationship and was supportive. She wanted to help her son escape to her father's ranch and wrote Don Feliciano a letter:

Dear Dad,

Greetings *desde* Nueva York! Greetings to Mom and the girls. Hope this letter finds you in good health. I wanted to tell you how miserable I feel in NYC. It's a big and cold city. Manolo continues to misbehave. I don't know how much more I can take and I wanna go home. But Joey needs help immediately. He is in love with an Italian girl, the daughter of Mr. Mario Capone, one of the most powerful men in New York City.

They are deeply in love, but Capone will not accept our son for his daughter. *Mi hijo* doesn't know that I am writing to you, but he has spoken about taking her to California. What do you think? Can you prepare a place for Joey and Rose? Can I go too? I'm sick and tired of Manolo.

Con mucho cariño y amor,
María

Don Feliciano's reply came three weeks later. He never liked Manolo and loved his daughter, but he did not want any daughter of his leaving her husband; yet he was willing to help Joey escape from New York. Maria read the letter with tears in her eyes. There was no escape for her. Joey received the news with mixed emotions. He wanted to go, but he knew how much his mother had suffered. He was uncertain about whether to go. He had witnessed the daily shouting and verbal abuses of his father. He stayed quiet, out of respect for his father, but he also felt he had gone too far.

Rose was hanging on a thread. She was formally committed to marry a man she did not love, but she was torn between obeying her father and loving Joey. It was too much for her to handle. The wedding was in six months, and Louie Jr. had already wanted more than kisses and hugs. Rose was living a daily emotional battle.

It was during these events in his life that Joey met Prof.Carlos Cintrón. The Department of Education had hired a professor of American and English literature to encourage young immigrants to get an education. But the Apostle, as he was called, did more than that.

Due to Joey's increasing interest in books, he had been taking a course in American and English literature in the public library at Lexington Avenue. His love for literature had developed immeasurably, and he wanted to read more about William Shakespeare, John Milton and Edgar Allan Poe.

The Apostle was a non-traditional teacher who transformed literature into a reality that went beyond ordinary situations. His students loved him, but his peers disliked his freestyle way of teaching the classics. The Professor felt he was ahead of his time, but every time he was in his presence, Joey received an inner peace that he had not experienced before. It was this peace that in a one-on-one conference with the Professor, Joey was able to have an encounter with the Spirit. After several weeks of internal introspection and more conversations with the Apostle, Joey decided to make drastic decisions that would help him move on with his life without regrets, knowing that he had received the inner strength and courage to make them happen.

Three months before the scheduled wedding, Joey decided to talk to Mr. Capone. He had found the necessary courage to confront the situation like a man. Thanks to the Apostle's guidance, he had learned that this was all part of a process, and there was no way that he would deviate from the path.

Winters in New York City were chillingly frightening. The roaring twenties had frozen the solar system in 1927. Although there was a warm stint at times, it seemed like an eternity before the mild and warm weather found its place between the hard brick homes and cold sidewalks. While Joey fluttered down the street towards his meeting with Capone, he felt the wind running through every cell of his body.

The Apostle's divine intervention was a determining factor in his final decision. He never told him what to do, but the process itself led him to decide the road to freedom. His mentor had spoken to him about a higher purpose in life, and he was looking forward to a life with a profound sense of meaning and direction. He helped him find his true identity.

After a long walk to Capone's, Joey breathed in and out and softly went in through the restaurant's front revolving door. He immediately spotted Mr. Capone in the lobby entrance and he gently and bravely interrupted a conversation between Capone and one of his employees.

"Mr. Capone, I'd like a few minutes of your valuable time."

"There is no need for a conversation. I am very busy right now and have made myself clear to your father." He quickly replied.

"Please, Mr. Capone; leave my father out of this. I believe that I can decide what to do with my life."

"So, you say, but you haven't decided wisely so far. You were told to stay away from Rose, and you haven't."

At this point, Capone pointed and carefully walked towards a small table in the back of the restaurant; Joey followed. Two of his associates accompanied them along the way. The brief walk to the table caught the attention of everyone at Capone's.

"Mr. Capone, I have decided to put my priorities in order."

"What does that have to do with my daughter?"

"Well, your precious daughter is a priority for me."

News through the restaurant traveled fast, and Rose's heart skipped a heartbeat when she heard that Joey was speaking to her father. He had once mentioned talking to her father, but this caught her by surprise.

"You know, Joey, you have a lot of guts coming into my restaurant. I own your father and your family. I don't know where you got the courage to see me. Personally, I got nothing against you, but I won't allow anyone to interfere in my plans to marry Rose to Louie Jr."

At this precise moment, one of his well-tailored employees said something to him in his ear.

"We must finish this conversation later. I have more serious business to take care of right now."

"Hear me out, please. I deeply love Rose, but I don't want to cause you or your family any problem. That's why I have decided to stop seeing your daughter. I wanted to tell you personally. Capone forced a smile, stood up, shook his hand, and left abruptly."

A day later, Rose and Joey met for the last time. Three of Capone's associates observed the couple at a distance. She was as beautiful as ever. He made it brief and simple. She was free to marry Righetti Jr., and he was going to visit the Island of Puerto Rico. She kept quiet and did not look at him throughout the ten-minute monologue. They hugged and parted their ways.

Joey wanted to encounter his roots, visit the Rio Blanco Hills and meet some of his father's relatives. It was necessary. He would come back, but he did not know when.

Maria was devastated the day Joey left to Puerto Rico. His co-workers arranged for someone to pick him up at the San Juan dock. Joey wanted to take his mother with him, but she did not want to be in his way. A month after her son left, she found the courage within herself and left Manolo and moved in with a sister in New Jersey who had also moved up East. She was still a young woman and wanted to begin a new life as well.

Manolo cursed the day she was born when he read her farewell letter. He had been away partying for the weekend and could care less anyway.

I put down the manuscript and saw that my fellow female passenger still slept. As she fell asleep, her head dropped on top of my shoulder. I stood still. I did not move and could smell her enchanting perfume. A few minutes later she woke up, and smiled when she found herself sleeping on my shoulder.

After I finished reading the story to myself, I sat back and tried to concentrate on the work ahead. It was a smooth landing, and Alma and I shook hands and said goodbye. Her smile was as wide as it could be, and I was tempted to ask her for her phone number but made an extreme effort not to and shifted my thoughts to the summer workshops. I hurriedly walked towards the New York City train station at the Kennedy Airport.

Twenty-one English teachers from New York City participated in the activity. I coordinated a symposium at a Puerto Rican town center in New York. Lalo Latorre, poet, Juan Hernández Rivera, poet, Dr. Juan Figueroa, essayist, and Janice Ortiz Cruz, short story writer read, presented and shared their experiences at the symposium. Latorre got the undivided attention of the New York audience when he began his presentation by reciting "My Graduation Speech":

"How are you? *¿Cómo estás?*"

"I don't know if I'm running *O si me fui pa*"

The event was televised by a PBS station in New York City and broadcasted to more than fifty cities throughout the United States of America. In 2001, the same New York Office hired me again. This time twenty-eight teachers participated in the one-week institute. Much to my surprise, teachers from other subject areas attended the workshop, as well as English and ESL teachers. One of the suggestions made was that I edit and create a textbook with reading and writing activities for students. From there on, I knew what my next project would be. I always wanted to be a published writer, and this was my opportunity.

In May of 2002, I was ready to make a proposal to a publishing house in San Juan. This was it. I developed a 14-page proposal that presented a four-chapter textbook for students in PR and the USA titled **<u>Latino /a Literature in the English Classroom</u>**. After years of reading presentations and essays on the subject, attending workshops and doing intense research on the subject matter, I was ready to make my elementary school teacher, Mrs. McGrath very proud. The book was culturally based and gave high school students the opportunity to make a connection to literature and build constructive bridges whenever they read, responded, and analyzed other traditional literatures in English.

The drive from Luquillo to San Juan was unusually swift and smooth. There was no traffic whatsoever, a miracle for this time of day. What would have been a one-hour drive took forty minutes. I turned the radio off about half-way to the meeting, and I prayed and meditated on how God had given me the opportunity to make it to this day after so many obstacles and barriers along the way. I thanked Him for His wisdom and direction. I made it to the business presentation with ten minutes to spare. I got out of the car and put my jacket on. I wasn't used to ties and jackets, but this was an exception. I breathed in and deeply out and walked into the publishing office. The publisher made me wait half-an-hour. I wiped the sweat that dripped down my forehead. At thirty past the hour, the secretary said the president, Leticia González, was ready to receive me.

Mrs. Gonzalez greeted me with a warm smile and a firm handshake. She was about my age, five-feet tall, petite and had short brown hair. She sat behind a brown business-like desk. She had pictures of her family all over the office. She began by thanking me for making it on time and for considering them as publishers for such an interesting project. I began by giving her a complete presentation of the project background. Then I went into details regarding the textbook and its intended audience. She listened. She interrupted my presentation and asked specific questions about the text, readings, and activities. After a three-hour presentation, Mrs. Gonzalez approved the project for the schools in Puerto Rico and the United States. She asked me for a few days before designing a contract. I left the office, got into my car, and prayed. It had been a long haul.

I drove home and shared the good news with my family. Maria and Joey were happy, and I was happy for them. I knew this was a good beginning and hoped to fulfill my purpose and destiny in my life.

THE FLORIDA EXPERIENCE

In the year 2000, Hispanics became the largest minority. When I saw the United States Census numbers, my heart dropped to my feet. Why? I knew that those numbers meant something, but there was no clear vision of what they signified. Suddenly, I heard voices from the past that suggested I expand my work with the Puerto Rican Diaspora and include Hispanics with other ethnic origins. The term Latino was all over the media. The largest minority became the question of my newfound journey.

After publishing my textbook, I expected invitations from universities, schools, and colleges, but none came. I never expected the drawback. The Department of Education in Puerto Rico (DE) verbally committed to considering the textbook for school-wide purchase, but they stalled and never came through with their proposal. It was a devastating blow to my dreams. My publisher had high expectations regarding the Department of Education's interest. When the Department did not come through with support, my publisher took a step back. I was left wandering what to do with my so-called visionary textbook.

As the days and weeks passed, I continued to be the only English teacher who authored a textbook on the Island of Puerto Rico but without an audience to appreciate its letters. I was frustrated, disappointed, and let down by those who had promised to help me along the pathway of my dreams. I visited a few schools and did a couple of reading presentations, but everyone asked if DE was supportive of the book. Most of the time I stuttered when responding to that question. It became a difficult question to answer.

Y2K also came with its share of national political turmoil. George W. Bush and Al Gore had a judicial face-off for the electoral votes for Florida. I was attracted to the news of the national political claim for the so-called Florida votes. The more I stared into the small screen to watch the day to day and moment to moment events surrounding the standout, the more I knew that Florida was somehow attached into my up-and-coming future.

I had visited the theme parks several times, but this time Florida was more than Mickey Mouse for me. It was on the political spectrum and mentioned as key state for the Presidential election. Hundreds of Puerto Rican families had already transitioned to Central Florida. Cities like Orlando, Tampa, Jacksonville, and Miami were capturing the attention of the new incoming Puerto Rican immigrant. Thousands of Puerto Rican retirees of the Northern states were purchasing homes in Central Florida, and their relatives on the Island were visiting and looking at Florida as an escape route from the economic and political mayhem on the Island.

My sisters-in-law left the Island in 2005. They settled North of Central Florida in Jacksonville. Both left with children and as single mothers barely had enough for the survival of their families. My nephews and niece struggled academically and dropped out of school. I will never forget a telephone call I got from Jose, my nephew. He spoke about racism, discrimination and not being able to adapt and adjust to school culture. Because he knew very little English, if any, he was bullied, ridiculed, and even mocked by educators. I tried to talk him into going back to class, but he never went back to school. I knew that Jose was not alone. He was part of a huge ESOL population that was not totally welcomed in the public school system. They simply did not expect the great number of students to flutter Florida schools. And the school system struggled to meet the expectations of the newfound immigrants. My lifetime work could make a difference. How?

In July of 2014, my family and I took our seventh family vacation to Orlando from Puerto Rico. My oldest son Joey was already living in his own apartment, and my wife and I wanted to spend some quality time with him before he got engaged or was too difficult to get for a family vacation. We went to the usual parks and made those crazy long lines to get on the rides. There was nothing extraordinary about the occasion. However, it felt different. Instead of staying in Orlando, we stayed in a nearby hotel in Kissimmee. After seven times, Orlando-Kissimmee started to look familiar.

As soon as we drove into the hotel, one of my wife's friend was there to greet her. Cassidy was a cancer patient, and my wife's friendship and prayers had made a difference in her illness. She was cancer free and wanted to thank her personally. I left them alone while my sons and I took up the luggage into the hotel room. It was early in the morning, and we already had messages in the front desk. It seemed like many of our Florida friends heard about our vacation through social media, and we were getting invited to picnics, barbecue parties and other social gatherings in the area.

We also received the opportunity to drive around the neighborhood. My curiosity about Florida took a different leap in 2000. And I wanted to take advantage that I was here in Florida to scout neighborhoods and look at school settings. We were not far from Osceola High School (OHS), and the school immediately came up on GPS. It was only minutes away from the hotel. When we drove by Osceola High School, I felt a magnet pulling me toward the school. I was a schoolteacher, but I worked at a school district in Puerto Rico and never thought of ever teaching again. Why did I feel like that? I couldn't get my eyes off the school. It looked brand new. It was my first sight of Osceola High School. Research validated the school as the largest in the District. I ran into some online news and found out that its football team was one of the top ten ranked high school teams in the state. Yet, academically OHS was a C. This was the school with the largest ESOL population in the Osceola School District.

We attended a couple of invitations and had a lot of fun during our eleven-day stay, and everywhere we went—our friends ended our visit with an invitation to move to Florida. There were people who went as far as prophesying that it was our time to move to Florida. It was scary! My wife started making plans, and I immediately got anxious. We had just spent a good portion of our savings on this vacation. Although we had vacationed here six times before, I never imagined moving here. For me, Florida was Walt Disney and Universal Studios. That was it!

Going back home meant affronting the future. As the plane flew over the Northern coastline of Puerto Rico, I could not help thinking that Florida was much more than seven magnificent vacations. My wife started making plans, and I counterattacked her plans in every which way possible. But she insisted and talked about it every second of the day.

One day, she came in from the gym and said:

"I am leaving for Florida soon!" She mumbled.

"How? Why? With whom?" I asked.

99

"By Faith!" She stated and hid from my sight before I responded.

I decided to go online and seek Florida teacher's certification. Maria was not fooling around. Surprisingly, I was certified in eight weeks. Maria started giving away furniture and selling some electrical appliances. One day I came home from work and the living room sofa was gone. The following week she gave away the microwave and other kitchen stuff. I stopped fighting her. Gradually, slowly, and steadfastly, the idea of moving to Florida became part of a perspective of a whole new thought that started finding its way into my mind. Why not Florida? Thousands of Hispanics were already there, and schools always needed teachers, especially ESOL teachers. It was a chance to make a difference, and I knew that there was place for my work there.

I did research on the educational system in Florida. My findings confirmed what I already knew. Hispanics were registering in great numbers, but they were failing and lagging academically. The acculturation process was met with a lack of understanding from those who had already settled in and from those who already lived in Florida. I started feeling a sense of purpose and urgency towards the matter. I knew that I was called to make a difference. This was an opportunity.

My wife focused on leaving the Island as soon as she could, and I said that I was moving too, but I still had part of my heart in Puerto Rico. I worked in a school district and had a very comfortable position as an English Academic Facilitator. My job was to train teachers and prepare them to meet the expectations of the Puerto Rico common core standards. It was new to all of us, but I enjoyed deciphering this complex academic system. I loved working with teachers and doing demonstration classes. It was a challenge, but it was something that came naturally. Although DE had not purchased my textbook, I had a job with them that transitioned my frustration into self-confidence. I put the book in the back of my mind and focused on assisting teachers. It was a magnificent job!

My wife insisted not to register our Josue in school in August of 2014. She knew that it was time to move to Florida, but I still did not quit my job. During the month of September, I received my Florida Teacher's Certificate, and I began searching for teaching jobs in Kissimmee. My wife left for Florida with our eight-year-old baby, Josue on September 27th, 2014. I was devastated when I left them at the airport. I wanted to leave, but I needed to secure a teaching position first.

Josue was born on September 22, 2005 at Ryder Hospital in Humacao, Puerto Rico. When my wife announced her pregnancy to Joey and me, I was 42 years old. I was at a crossroads in my career and my personal life. We lived in Rio Blanco, Naguabo. The "Rio Blanco" was an impressive "white river" that ran down from Puerto Rico's "El Yunque" (a national rainforest). Our new house had the view at a distance, and I used to sit on the porch and glance at the river for long minutes every day. After nineteen years into our marriage, we finally had a new house, but the mortgage payments were a bit out of my range, and I started doubting the so-called blessing my house had been just a year before. The announcement came with excitement and jubilee, but I also wondered how we could provide a good quality of life for the up-and-coming baby. What a contrast, but it was a blessing because I focused and turned the "goal setting" control again. There was no room for retirement. Josue was my newfound inspiration.

Maria moved in with our nephew Jose. While I continued job hunting, she registered Josue in an elementary school in Jacksonville. I spoke to them every night. And started seriously thinking about moving to Florida. It was a risky move. I was 50 years of age, and I knew that moving to Florida meant teaching in the classroom. For six years, I worked as a teacher-trainer in Puerto Rico. Teaching full-time again was really going to be a challenge. I loved teaching, but I had gotten comfortable as a teacher-trainer. It was an office job. I took long breaks, and sometimes took "overtime" lunches.

Teaching in Florida was not going to be easy, but I decided to accept the challenge. At mid-life, I needed a test of character. This was either going to make me or break me. I ran right into the test and focused on the steps that I needed to take to transition into Kissimmee, Florida. First, I found a teaching job available at Osceola High School. That was the school that I could not get my eyes off on my last vacation to Orlando. I looked at their registration numbers and read that almost two third of the students were of Hispanic origin. Second, I sent my resume to the school and in a week got a call, was interviewed, and offered a position. The Assistant Principal stated that they were looking for a Hispanic male role model. Wow! That was my calling. Last, I quit my job in Puerto Rico and bought a one-way airline ticket to Jacksonville, Florida. I was two plus hours from Kissimmee, but I knew that I was getting closer to my purpose.

My oldest son drove me to the airport that early October Monday morning. It was a cold tropical and windy day. The clouds were gray, and the sun seemed to be hiding behind one of the thick dark clouds in the sky. I was focused yet tentative--not because of the decision but because of the perils that I was putting my family through. We were moving to Florida with very little cash and zero savings.

When I went to the DE teacher's retirement office to pick up my retirement check, the clerk showed me a memo recently sent to them from the Governor himself. All pensions and retirement checks were being canceled. The government was bankrupt! I almost had a heart attack. It was time to leave. My family deserved better.

It was time to say goodbye. I drove up to meet my firstborn. Joey cried as he hugged me goodbye. He was in his mid-twenties, but I held back the tears. It was heartbreaking. I was leaving the Island, but I was also leaving my oldest son behind as well. He was a Youth Minister at a mega-church in the Metropolitan area and loved his work with teenagers. My heart was torn, divided, shattered and at peace all at once.

Maria and Josue moved into a one-room apartment in my nephew's apartment in Jacksonville not Kissimmee. I had a job in progress in Kissimmee, but I did not have a place to live in yet. I asked numerous people about where to rent, but all I got were links to different residential and apartment complexes. All those who encouraged us to move to Kissimmee did not answer our telephone calls. There was even an ex-cop friend of ours who worked in a car dealership that offered to help us get a vehicle once we moved to Florida, but every time I called, he asked me to identify myself. After several calls, I got the message.

Truth was that I had no money whatsoever. I held on to Maria's faith. Her Florida drive was like a hurricane that expressed itself in her desire to walk through a path decisively and passionately. She encouraged me to move by Faith, and that I did. She constantly cheered me up and kept me focused on the task ahead. We were going to start from scratch. No home. No car. No money. We even discussed the possibility of moving into a homeless shelter.

I landed in Jacksonville two weeks after my Maria arrived. Jose went to pick me up at the airport. Although I nailed a teaching position at OHS, it was still weeks before my background check and fingerprints cleared. Or at least I thought I had all that time. Maria and Josue were happy to see me. And I was elated to be back with my wife and Josue. The next few days were all about my time with them. I knew that at some point I would be leaving them. Kissimmee was in Central Florida, but I did not know anyone and did not have a place to live there yet.

Just a few days after I temporarily settled in Jacksonville, I received a call from the Assistant Principal at Osceola High School. I was hired.

"Fingerprints were cleared today, Mr. Hernandez."

"Wow! That was fast." I replied.

"They usually take several weeks to clear, but yours came back good to go in a week. It looks like somebody wants you down here asap."

"I agree."

"When can you start, Mr. Hernandez?" Mr. Johnson immediately asked.

"I still don't have a place to stay in the area." I said.

"Well, we can only give you a few more days." He quickly added.

"I'll get it done, Mr. Johnson. I'll be ready."

"I'll call you back in two days with a beginning date." He said as he abruptly hung up the phone.

For the first time since the year 2000, I finally understood that Florida was here to stay. I looked at my wife and shared the good news. I had a job. All I needed now was a place to stay. I called friends, family, and anyone I knew that could help me get a room, apartment or a space where I could sleep. Once again, there were no return calls and no information from anyone. Two days later, there was a minor breakthrough. My sister had a friend in Kissimmee, and she called the owner of the room, and they agreed to hold it for me. It was only a room to sleep in. Another gentleman slept in the other bedroom, and we were going to share the bathroom and kitchen. Not my typical living arrangements, but I saw it as a door that started to open.

When Mr. Johnson called again, it was to tell me that they expected me at the school in a week. I started getting ready for the journey. A few days later, I said goodbye to Maria and Josue. Until I was able to rent an apartment, they stayed in Jacksonville. I called Mike Rodriguez, a friend of mine from Lake Mary, and he agreed to pick me up in Orlando and drive me to my new dwelling place.

On the two hours plus on the Greyhound that day, I thought of all the unknowns in this new challenge. I didn't know anyone in the area, but I knew that it had to be Kissimmee, and it had to be Osceola High School. So many questions. But I repeated and repeated to myself on the bus, that this was part of a plan, and I was here to transform education. How? I had Faith, but doubt creeped into my mind from time to time. That was probably the longest two and a half hours of my life.

I arrived at the Orlando Greyhound station a bit after 8:00 pm. I called Mike. He was already on his way. We hugged and started the final stage of my first sight of the real Kissimmee. Seven vacations, but this was the beginning of something beyond my wildest imagination. And it was no vacation.

Mike put the address in the GPS, and we took off to the one bedroom that I was being offered to rent. It was small, just a small television, a closet, and a shared bathroom with my housemate, Jorge. We were immediately introduced, and he seemed like a nice guy. After the formal introductions, it was time for me to make a down payment on the room. The landlord said that I owed her $575.00. I stalled and kept quiet while I thought on how to tell her that I only had $150.00. in my pocket.

"Ma'am, I have $150.00 dollars, but I can only give you $100.00." I stated.

"Sir, what are you saying? Do you know how many people are interested in this room? And we held it for you because you were recommended." She replied.

"Ma'am, I have $150.00 dollars, but I can only give you $100.00." I repeated.

"I am a teacher, and I will not get paid until the end of the month." I added.

I repeated the same statement three times. The third time she called the owner and put him on the phone. I spoke with him and reassured him that I would pay him as soon as I got paid. He insulted me, but I kept my cool until he asked to speak to the landlord again. I overheard him ask the landlord about my character. Finally, and only after I repeated the same story to him several times did he say that I could pay him $100 and pay him the rest later. It was a miracle of Faith in action. Now, I knew that I was in the right time in the right place.

The next day I woke up at 5:00 am sharp. I got up, got on my knees, and prayed. This was the first day of the rest of my life. I thanked God for bringing me here and asked HIM for focus and courage. It was 25 minutes to get to the bus stop. Then another 25-

minute walk after I got off the bus and to the school. I loved the bus ride because it gave me a scope of the people in the area.

Although the five-mile distance from my room was merely a ten-minute drive, it took more than two hours to catch two buses and walk fifty minutes to get to OHS. First day of school for me, but it was the first week of October, and almost the end of the first quarter. When I walked into the school, I was immediately rushed in to see one of the school secretaries. She put a contract in front of me and warned me that I could be fired in five days. She mumbled some words after, but I could only hear her say that I could be fired in five days. I almost choked in silence, but I gathered my thoughts quickly and signed without saying a word.

I met the Assistant Principal who interviewed me on the phone. Mr. Johnson was a jovial and enthusiastic administrator. He greeted me and gave me some hurried instructions about the school and my job. He added that I was going to observe a teacher for two days, and I would take over her classes after that. That was not the original agreement. I kept quiet and really did not understand the working culture at OHS. They were already not keeping the verbal agreement. I was supposed to teach Honor's English and four ESOL classes. Instead, I got English Language Learners that were neither ESOL nor Honor's English. This was on the job training, and I needed to focus and learn fast.

English Speakers of Other Languages (ESOL) students were registering in Central Florida schools at unprecedented rates. With each new semester and academic year, schools **were working comprehensively to make space to accommodate the increasing student growth and the incoming ESOL student population.** These students were part of the greatest migration movement in current history. As a result, the demographics of schools changed drastically. I was right in the middle of an academic storm. I looked forward to the task. It was an ideal situation for me with more questions than answers, but I loved the challenge. They promised to give me ESOL students the following semester, and I finally got the students I was hired to teach two months after my arrival.

It was difficult! The Florida educational system was designed for students to prepare and pass district and state standardized exams. What we taught, what students read and the examinations they took were already pre-ordained. I had heard about the Common Core, but this was scrupulous. How was I going to make a difference in a system like this one? Although I came with close to 30 years of teaching experience, I was a new English Language Arts teacher for school purposes, and my experience was only relevant for classroom teaching. I came here to make a difference in the macro, but I focused and reiterated my energies for the micro.

On the very first day of class, I received a classroom visit from my administrator. He took pictures of my board work and scrutinized every evidence of my classroom teaching. This was beyond my imagination, but I continued to come in agreement with Maria and my sons that this was part of a greater purpose. Every day I worked late and tried hard to understand how to align and decipher the Common Core. Towards the end of that month and the first one in Florida, I had an experience that lifted me up from the ashes of my doubts about the whole Florida experience. Two female colleagues walked into my classroom. It was after 6:00 pm, and I wasn't expecting any visitors. When they saw me, they both laughed. I was startled because I did not know any of them. I asked.

"Is everything ok?"

"You are not going to believe this!" one of the ladies stated.

"I don't understand." I answered back.

"You were one of my college professors back in Puerto Rico." One of the two said.

"What?"

"That's right. I'm Sandra Rodriguez."

"Of course, how could I forget you?"

"You remember. This is Mrs. Feliciano."

"Nice to meet you, Ms. Feliciano."

"She is the ESOL Compliance person."

"Wow! We laughed because you had hair back then." She giggled.

I could not help thinking it was three weeks since I started teaching, and my ESOL coach had not been to my classroom to greet me or share any ideas and strategies. Although I was a veteran teacher, everything at OHS was new to me, but I didn't want to embarrass her in front of Sandra.

Sandra worked in the Osceola School District, and she visited my room from time to time. What were the possibilities of running into an ex-student from Puerto Rico, who now was my supervisor as well? This was an understanding that Purpose was the driving force in my relocation process in Kissimmee. Sandra helped me feel at ease and offered to provide technical assistance immediately.

There were more than two dozen Hispanic teachers at OHS, but they were not friendly or welcoming at all. It was an interesting experience. I tried hard to befriend a few, but they seemed distant and cautious. I walked the huge campus in search of a friend but found none. It took me a while to understand that for some inexplicable reason—the acculturation process and the ordeals of a new culture worked against the common values of solidarity and friendship. I started to understand why those who knew me disappeared once I moved in the area. Why would they pick-up the phone to help if they barely had enough to make ends meet?

There were two exceptions to what I had experienced in my relocation process. There were two colleagues that made me feel at home and truly welcomed. Dr. Maria Torrey and her husband, Mr. Torrey. There were days that I did not even have lunch, and Mr. Torrey offered me soup and coffee, almost daily. Dr. Torrey was a scholar in Puerto Rican literature. Finally, someone whom I could talk and relate to. She shared her doctoral dissertation with me. When I told her about the class I created at the University of Puerto Rico, we developed a bond, and mutual respect. Her work encouraged me to continue moving forward in my quest to make a difference at OHS. They were God sent people who gave me enough courage and sustenance to make it through those first months at OHS.

I attended Student Advisory Council (SAC) meetings. These were parent, teacher, student, and administrator meetings where projects were presented and approved through the SAC committee. I had an idea of presenting a proposal. I needed a proposal to build a foundation for the years ahead. That's when I created Creating Lifelong Writers (CLW). In the public school system in Florida, there was hardly any reading and/or discussion of authentic and relevant literature that represented students as a distinct and unique culture. Central Florida High School's demographics changed drastically in the last 20 years. The educational system was supposed to serve the needs of a multi-ethnic, multi-cultural student body through diverse programs and activities, but it wasn't.

Creating Lifelong Writers (CRL) was an initiative to ignite such programs and activities. I underwent the task of inviting the internationally acclaimed author Esmeralda Santiago. In Latino/a letters, she was second to none, and her story was similar to the stories of the recently arrived ESOL kids. Santiago relocated from Puerto Rico to New York City in the late 1960's with her mom, six brothers and sisters. Her mom's resilience and drive to keep her family tight knit and focused helped her overcome personal struggles, extreme impoverished conditions and language barriers to send her on an academic path to Julliard and to Harvard University.

After an intense debate, the SAC approved CLW. The majority of SAC was against CLW, and a very influential parent did not understand the validity of CLW. In the end, the Principal intervened, and the SAC voted to approve the project. It was my first major battle. In CLW, Esmeralda Santiago constructed a bridge from her personal journey to academic success which allowed students from all ethnic backgrounds to empower themselves with a live interactive media conference with one of the best-selling authors in the United States. The purpose of CLW was to enhance teaching instruction to the so-called Common Core. Santiago's story provided insight into the college and career readiness skills required by universities and colleges today.

More than 600 students participated in this unique and historic event with Esmeralda Santiago. Students were able to ask questions and make comments via live streaming. It was truly a magnificent event. We also purchased 50 books from the best-selling author. The OHS administration supported and promoted the event, and the turnout was a major academic success. At the end of that school year (2014-2015) and as a result, I was invited to revise and transform curriculum at the Osceola School District. I was asked to be part of a committee that would edit and improve the curriculum map that ultimately impacted ESOL students. This was why I came to Florida.

ABOUT THE AUTHOR

Manuel Hernandez was born and grew up in North Tarrytown, New York in 1963. His parents moved back to their home country, Puerto Rico during the beginning of Manuel's pre-adolescence. At the age of fifteen, he moved back to New York City. That was the beginning of his revolving door experience which lasted for more than forty years.

He graduated with honors from Pedro Falu High School, Rio Grande, Puerto Rico in 1981. He went on and did his B.A. at the University of Puerto Rico (UPR) in Education and graduated with honors in 1985. In 1986, he became a teacher and completed his Master's Degree with Honors in 1994 from Herbert H. Lehman College (CUNY) in The Bronx, New York. After completing his Master's, he returned to Puerto Rico and worked for more than 20 years in the public high schools. He also taught and did administrative work in his alma mater, UPR, Rio Piedras. He is an author of four books, Latino/a Literature in the English Classroom, 2003, Living the Kingdom with Purpose, 2012, and the Coming to America (4 edition series). He has been an English Language Arts Instructor since 2014 at Osceola High School in Kissimmee, Florida. He is the proud husband of Maria Ortiz Rodriguez and father of two boys, Jose Manuel and Josue Esteban.

ABOUT THE GRAPHIC ARTIST AND AUTHOR

Maria Victoria Calderon-Torrey was born on the Lower East Side in New York City from Puerto Rican parents that migrated during the early 1950's. After graduating from Queen's College (CUNY) with an education degree during the seventies, she traveled throughout the United States, and worked in several teaching positions, which included English as a Second Language (ESL) to Cuban Refugees in the 1980's, as well as Bilingual Reading Recovery in the "Southwest" (Texas and California) in the nineties.

While living in the Southwest, Maria Victoria (Vicky) continued graduate work at the University of San Francisco: earning a Master of Arts degree in "Teaching English as a Second Language" and a education doctorate (Ed.D) in "International Multicultural Education" specializing in Puerto Rican culture. Longing to serve the community of the beloved culture of her parents, she moved to Central Florida with her husband, who also served as a teacher in Osceola County since 2001. Both Vicky and her husband Les Paul work as professional photographers, having contributed photographs for children's books that support literacy learning (Candid Collection/Dominie Press and Bebop Books/Lee & Low). Her doctoral dissertation, "Puerto Rican Authors: Voicing Identity in Puerto Rican Literature", was published in 2003, but she continued to study and earn two additional graduate degrees from Nova Southeastern University: with an Educational Leadership Ed.S and Master of Science in "Instructional Technology and Distance Education".

Made in United States
Orlando, FL
12 February 2022